ROUTLEDGE LIBRARY EDITIONS:
EDUCATION IN ASIA

Volume 2

CHINA'S SCHOOLS IN FLUX

CHINA'S SCHOOLS IN FLUX

Report by the State Education Leaders Delegation, National Committee on United States–China Relations

Edited by
RONALD N. MONTAPERTO AND
JAY HENDERSON

LONDON AND NEW YORK

First published in 1979 by M.E. Sharpe Inc.

This edition first published in 2018
by Routledge
2 Park Square, Milton Park, Abingdon, Oxon OX14 4RN

and by Routledge
711 Third Avenue, New York, NY 10017

Routledge is an imprint of the Taylor & Francis Group, an informa business

© 1979 M.E. Sharpe Inc.

All rights reserved. No part of this book may be reprinted or reproduced or utilised in any form or by any electronic, mechanical, or other means, now known or hereafter invented, including photocopying and recording, or in any information storage or retrieval system, without permission in writing from the publishers.

Trademark notice: Product or corporate names may be trademarks or registered trademarks, and are used only for identification and explanation without intent to infringe.

British Library Cataloguing in Publication Data
A catalogue record for this book is available from the British Library

ISBN: 978-1-138-30826-8 (Set)
ISBN: 978-1-315-14674-4 (Set) (ebk)
ISBN: 978-1-138-31015-5 (Volume 2) (hbk)
ISBN: 978-1-138-50541-4 (Volume 2) (pbk)
ISBN: 978-1-315-14656-0 (Volume 2) (ebk)

Publisher's Note
The publisher has gone to great lengths to ensure the quality of this reprint but points out that some imperfections in the original copies may be apparent.

Disclaimer
The publisher has made every effort to trace copyright holders and would welcome correspondence from those they have been unable to trace.

China's Schools in Flux

REPORT BY THE STATE EDUCATION LEADERS DELEGATION,
NATIONAL COMMITTEE ON UNITED STATES–CHINA RELATIONS

Ronald N. Montaperto
Jay Henderson,
Editors

Ralph W. Tyler
William A. Delano
Gregory R. Anrig
Adrienne Y. Bailey
Grace C. Baisinger
Mary F. Berry
Marlin L. Brockette
Frank B. Brouillet
Calvin M. Frazier
Virginia Macy
Wilson Riles
Thomas C. Schmidt
Louis R. Smerling
Lillian Weber
Donald Ferguson

© M. E. Sharpe Inc. 1979
901 North Broadway
White Plains, New York 10603

All rights reserved. No part of this publication may be reproduced or transmitted, in any form or by any means, without permission

First published in the U.S.A. 1979
First published in the U.K. 1980

Published by
THE MACMILLAN PRESS LTD
London and Basingstoke
Associated companies in Delhi
Dublin Hong Kong Johannesburg Lagos
Melbourne New York Singapore Tokyo

Printed in the United States of America by
MALLOY LITHOGRAPHING, INC.
Ann Arbor, Michigan

This book is sold subject to the standard conditions of the Net Book Agreement

CONTENTS

Preface   vii
Jay Henderson

China's Education in Perspective   1
Ronald N. Montaperto

Organization and Structure   39
Thomas C. Schmidt

Decision Making   60
Frank B. Brouillet

Curriculum   77
Gregory R. Anrig

Admissions   92
Louis R. Smerling

Work and Study   106
Calvin M. Frazier and
Wilson Riles

Early Childhood Education   124
Lillian Weber

Family and Community Involvement   135
Grace C. Baisinger and
Virginia Macy

Relevance to American Needs   150
Mary F. Berry

Conclusions   163
Ralph W. Tyler

Appendices
Itinerary   175
Members of the Delegation   186

PREFACE

Jay Henderson

National Committee on U.S.-China Relations

The State Education Leaders Delegation traveled to the People's Republic of China in October 1977 under the auspices of the National Committee on United States-China Relations and at the invitation of the Chinese Ministry of Education. The purpose of the visit was to observe and discuss the new directions of China's schools.

The Delegation was composed of leaders in the field of American education mainly at the state level, where primary responsibility for administration of elementary and secondary schools rests in the United States. Ralph W. Tyler, who served as delegation leader, is one of America's foremost philosophers of education. His titles, past and present, include dean of the School of Education at the University of Chicago, director of the Chicago program of the Center for the Study of Democratic Institutions, senior consultant with Science Research Associates in Chicago, and director emeritus of the Center for Advanced Study in the Behavioral Sciences at Stanford. William A. Delano, counsel for Global Perspectives in Education in New York and an Executive Committee member of the National Committee on U.S.-China Relations, acted as deputy leader. Other members included the Assistant Secretary for Education of the U.S. Department of Health, Education and Welfare; six state commissioners of education and superintendents of public instruction; the president and the president-elect of the

National Association of State Boards of Education; the Presidents of the National and California Parent Teachers Associations; and the director of the Workshop Center for Open Education at City College in New York. In addition to these fourteen educators, the delegation was accompanied by a professor of political science at Indiana University whose major field of study is China's youth; the deputy director of the Office of East Asian and Pacific Programs of the Bureau of Educational and Cultural Affairs of the Department of State; and the author of this preface, a program associate of the National Committee on United States-China Relations.

On the morning of October 28 the delegation arrived in Peking from Karachi, Pakistan, after a night flight across the Himalayas. We departed China on November 14 from Kwangchou (Canton) by train for Hong Kong. During the intervening eighteen days the group visited four preschool centers; three primary schools; one middle school; six colleges, universities, and vocational schools; two school-run factories; the Shanghai Children's Palace; and the homes of eight Chinese families with school-age children. The delegation held eight seminars with Chinese education specialists; over 100 people attended the one in Peking. The discussions usually pertained to the administration of education in China (in which case Chinese educators answered questions put by our delegation) or the administration of education in the United States (in which we responded to questions asked by Chinese). In Peking there was also a 90-minute meeting with Minister of Education Liu Hsi-yao, and in Nanking the delegation spent nearly two hours discussing provincial education with Madame Fang Fei, the deputy chief of education for Kiangsu Province.

The delegation left for China at an interesting time. Media in the United States carried the news that a major effort was freshly underway to get China's schools "back to the basics." To illustrate, only days before our arrival more than 20 million young Chinese eligible to enter college had been given the news that for the first time in more than a decade everyone who applied for college would be required to take entrance examinations and be judged primarily by academic skills and not by class background (the predominant criterion of the 1966-1976 era). Some 5.7 million candidates took the examination in early December in competition for 300,000 enrollment slots.

Educators we met in China assured us that academic excellence was to be reintroduced as a primary goal of education in China. The new campaign was designed to moderate the degree to which education policies had been politicized during and since the Cultural Revolution of 1966-69. We were told that the philosophy of "putting politics in command" had been pushed to destructive ends during the previous decade and that, as a result, academic standards had fallen so low as to allow China to "waste an entire generation of its intellects." Yet our delegation saw evidence that both schools of thought were still very much in contention. The Chinese called this conflict of ideas the "red vs. expert" debate, or contradiction.

On the one hand, many of the "red" ideas which had emerged during the Cultural Revolution were still being praised. "May 7" cadre schools (where white collar workers and bureaucrats engage in manual labor and study Marxism, Leninism, and Mao Tse-tung thought) were being retained; so were "July 21" Universities (factory-run universities), and minority quotas for college entrants from remote areas. Urban youth were still being sent to the countryside after graduation from middle school (although in not quite as great a number as before), medical schools were continuing to graduate paramedics, known as barefoot doctors, and teachers and professors were still obligated to engage periodically in manual labor. It may be that certain politically inspired education policies will continue to have a place in China's schools so long as they have a basis in necessity. At the Nanking Power School, for instance, we discovered that the school's factories produced enough profit every year, 300,000 yuan, to finance almost entirely the school's annual 340,000-yuan budget. Thus, a decision to depoliticize this school's curriculum would have many expensive implications for China's education budget.

On the other hand, the anti-"Gang of Four" campaign seemed to be carrying with it a great tide of new "expert" ideas in education which would serve to raise the standards of education quality. Admissions policies were clearly undergoing such revisions. Discipline was being restored to schools. Teacher's titles were on the way back. Layman-led revolutionary committees in day-to-day charge of schools were being dissolved and replaced by more traditional bodies headed by school officials. Academic courses with clear-cut curricula and tough examinations were back. Although grades and degrees had not yet been reintroduced, they were under consideration. The list of these reforms was long. In fact, it kept getting longer as we were in China and has continued to grow since we returned home.

The papers which follow represent the views of the members of the delegation. The decision to write this report was made at a briefing of the State Education Leaders Delegation held two months before our departure. We chose to prepare each section of our report individually, thereby taking advantage of the clearly separate interests of our delegation members. (The PTA representatives, for example, could use their special experience and talents to evaluate similar aspects of China's education system.) Most of the views reported here were formed after we began our short stay in the People's Republic of China. Far from being definitive, therefore, they are limited by the narrowness of our sampling, by the fact that what we saw was what we were shown, by the variety of our individual reactions, and, finally, by the realization that few things are so constant as change in China's education system.

Ronald Montaperto's chapter, "China's Education in Perspective," is intended to provide a definition of China's historical educational goals and a chronology of education history since the founding of the PRC in 1949. Thomas Schmidt's paper on "Organization and Structure" describes the network of administrative offices which make up China's educational bureaucracy and introduces several educational functions which are either entirely new and previously unheard of outside China, or which have been revived in the wake of the fall of the "Gang of Four." Frank Brouillet's chapter on "Decision Making" describes the preeminent role of the Chinese Communist Party. Gregory Anrig provides a detailed account of the nature of the new curriculum. Louis Smerling's description of "Admissions" processes lists the steps which Chinese children from preschool to university must take to gain entrance, explains how quotas for minorities and scholarships for low income Chinese families work, and examines the function of political evaluations in the admission of students to schools. In their chapter on "Work and Study," Calvin Frazier and Wilson Riles discuss the relationship of the school to China's goal of becoming a developed country and provide examples of how schools are now using practical work experience to reinforce the theoretical knowledge of the classroom. Lillian Weber's "Early Childhood Education" incorporates the view of several members of the delegation that rote learning is not the only method of instruction in China, as some previous American visitors to China have reported. Grace Baisinger and Virginia Macy outline the nature of the Chinese family's and the community's involvement with local schools, concluding that involvement is minimal and controlled by the schools, that parents are the least involved of all parties concerned, that grandparents often play a larger role than might be expected, and that the community is allowed to support but not to challenge school policies. Mary Berry provides her observations on the relevance (or lack thereof) of the Chinese experience to America's educational needs. Ralph Tyler summarizes the conclusions of the entire delegation and offers his own observations on the efficacy of China's approach to education in the post-Mao era.

The members of the State Education Leaders Delegation and the National Committee on U.S.-China Relations wish to express their appreciation to the individuals and organizations whose combined efforts made their trip to China possible: to the Chinese Ministry of Education for its invitation and its generosity and graciousness as host; to the Office of Education in the U.S. Department of Health, Education and Welfare for covering the costs of the delegation's international travel; and to the Johnson Foundation for twice providing its Wingspread Conference Center in Racine, Wisconsin, for the delegation's two-day briefing prior to departure and for its subsequent debriefing.

CHINA'S EDUCATION IN PERSPECTIVE

Ronald N. Montaperto

Indiana University

China, like all societies, is informed by a set of values that determines where and how to allocate social resources. Chinese values are expressed in an ideology based upon the ideas of Marx, Engels, Lenin, and Mao Tse-tung. They reflect, therefore, both a commitment to universal norms and goals derived from Marxism, and a specific application of these overreaching concepts to conditions in China. The key, of course, is revolution: the world revolution and the Chinese revolution. By building its own revolution, China reaffirms its commitment to world social change.

The ideology of revolution has many implications for Chinese education. For example, we are told that real learning can occur only through direct experience with concrete reality. As individuals move through life, their various perceptions enable them to form impressions of their environment. As perceptions increase in number, they are combined to form conceptualizations or concepts that serve to order the world. Ultimately concepts must be further combined and interrelated to form theories that will enable the individual to participate effectively in life. If the learner does this, then Chinese ideology holds that real knowledge has been attained and the individual is capable of effecting revolutionary social change. In other words, in the Chinese view there is a direct relationship between theory and practice; revolutionary education must by definition embrace both of these dimensions. Theory leads the individual to a certain form of practice in the concrete world and it is that practice which validates or invalidates the theory.[1]

A second important implication for the idea of learning is the assumption that education reflects the needs and preferences of whatever social classes dominate society at a particular time. In capitalist societies, perceptions, conceptualizations, and theories serve to reinforce the values of capitalism, while in socialist societies, education inevitably must offer a different set of imperatives. The class or classes that control the sources of economic productivity create a system of education that justifies and extends their control. In the Chinese view, all education is ultimately political.[2]

If all that we have said is true, then the term "education" refers to a wide range of experiences that transcend the formal classroom environment. In this larger sense, society itself provides the broad context in which real learning occurs. Schools, teachers, administrators — in fact, the whole complex of explicitly educational institutions — are of extreme importance in imparting a certain body of facts and theories. But the utility of these relatively narrow experiences is seriously qualified unless they are confirmed in the context of the whole society. In this sense the purpose of social organization in the People's Republic of China is to create an environment in which citizens receive exposure to the perceptions, concepts, and theories that will bring them to view the world through socialist eyes.

Society and social relations are loci of education. Schools are viewed as but one feature of the larger society, and their role, apart from imparting factual knowledge, is both to inculcate the socialist values of Chinese society and to reinforce the perceptions of collectivism gained by students in their daily lives.

A final observation is that Chinese ideology implies that all human beings are capable of attaining rational knowledge — learning — if they are instructed in the proper manner. While the Chinese acknowledge differences in intelligence, talent, temperament, and individual preferences for different types of subjects, they also hold that all men can acquire socialist consciousness. The life experiences of a proletarian may make it easier for a member of that class to achieve this, but it is also possible for a former landlord or factory owner to be reeducated or remolded. All that is required is that the person be exposed to appropriate perceptions and concepts. The general assumption is that all individuals have some contribution to make and that it is education in both the broad sense of social relations and in the more narrow sense of the classroom that makes this possible.

All of the contributors to this volume acknowledge these salient points of Chinese ideology, even if only implicitly. However, it is important that they be emphasized here because it is along precisely these dimensions that the Chinese distinguish the goals, methods, organization, and operation of their educational system from that of other countries. To understand this is to take the first step toward understanding education in the People's Republic of China in its own terms.

The Beginnings: Historical Perspective

On October 1, 1949, the proclamation of the People's Republic of China signaled the virtual completion of the "Liberation" phase of the Chinese revolution. There followed a period of consolidation, reconstruction, and reform, and then a transition to socialist or at least collective forms of ownership of the means of production. Naturally, education changed as well.

However, the leadership was confronted by a problem of staggering proportions. The Anti-Japanese War and the Civil War with the Kuomintang (Nationalists) had left China's economy in desperate straits. While the Chinese Communist Party (CCP) did inherit the structure of a viable educational system, they lacked the resources to make it work. There was a problem of means.

Second, and of greater importance, the CCP had to face the fact that the scale of the educational system inherited from the

Kuomintang era was simply of insufficient size to meet the
needs of the new nation with its commitment to industrialization
and rapid increase in provision of goods and services. While a
system was in place, and while students were eager, the new
government could not begin to accommodate them all in the institutions available. Also, many of the teachers at all levels
were not totally committed to the new regime, although most
were not overtly hostile. In fact, in the Party's view they represented a segment of the population that had to be won over to
the revolutionary cause. Thus, the CCP had to solve problems
of scale.

If the resources available to the CCP were scarce or inadequate, they were also distributed unevenly throughout China's
vast landmass. At the beginning of the twentieth century, when
China began to develop a modern educational system, the new
institutions were located in the traditional cultural and political
centers of Peking, Shanghai, Nanking, and Canton. Modern education began and developed along a north-south axis in the
eastern and central portions of the country. While some colleges and universities were located in the interior, they were
found mainly in the Yangtze river valley, where the river provided access and relative ease of communication. A similar
pattern obtained with respect to primary and middle schools.
Lower-level units grew up around the centers of higher education and served essentially as feeder schools for the colleges
and universities in the larger cities. The primary and secondary schools located outside of these areas were concentrated in
the provincial capitals and market towns, and many were run
with the benefit of foreign assistance derived mainly from mis-
sionary sources. The 85 percent of China's population that re-
sided in the rural countryside did not have easy access to the
educational system. Thus, for the CCP, rebuilding the educational system required the establishment of new schools at all
levels in areas that had always lacked such facilities.[3]

In addition to the material problems of physical plant and
capital construction, the CCP was also forced to confront two
other situations with historical roots. Much of the country's

"modern" educational establishment had been created and developed with foreign aid and assistance. From the turn of the century until 1933, Chinese officials had favored the American model for all levels. American educators taught, lectured, and helped to plan the curriculums of many of the major universities; they also had a voice in the construction of the system of primary and secondary education. In some cases this aid and advice was direct, but more often the practices established at one university, secondary school, or primary school simply diffused through society. The result was that by 1932 the system had a distinctly American stamp, with the individual student having considerable say in the construction of his major field of study. Similarly, because the liberal arts were strongly entrenched, secondary schools frequently guided their college preparatory students in that direction.[4]

Then, during the 1931-32 period the Kuomintang regime having established something approximating a stable political base, turned its attention to problems of education. The League of Nations sent a team to China to survey conditions and reported, as the Nationalists had hoped they would, that the European university system with its emphasis on specialization was more suited to China's needs. Specialization would facilitate planning and ease problems of economic development. The point to be taken here is that despite the manifest competence of Chinese educators, education at all levels was enervated because of its reliance upon foreign theories and methods. Although the Chinese themselves administered the system and although they established a commendable record, they were working with concepts, theories, and procedures that were imported. In effect, China's educational establishment did not grow in response to Chinese needs, but rather represented Chinese acceptance of what certain non-Chinese experts felt to be most appropriate for the country at the time. The Chinese did not learn to control their own educational world and the CCP had to find a means of dealing with this situation.[5]

The second problem grew out of the first and is seen in the splits and divisions that characterized China's intellectual circles. Early in the present century many youths studied abroad, especially in the United States and Japan. When they returned they formed the faculties and research staffs of the major universities. They also had established lines of communication which made it easier for them to have their students follow in their footsteps and undertake foreign study. Understandably, the better students attempted to enter this type of university; for identical reasons, secondary schools sought to establish impressive records of sending students to such institutions. Eventually, this reached down to the primary levels with the result that a structure of elite schools grew up which offered the greatest chance of advancement after graduation. In fact, graduates of this elite system moved into the best positions in business, industry, and government during the period prior to 1949.

At the same time, much larger numbers of students were attending the less prestigious schools at all levels in the provinces and, owing to the lack of access to the relatively small number of professional positions, they received their secondary or university degrees but often virtually nothing else. They were not able to compete effectively in the employment market and only rarely could they find positions for which their education had trained them. In desperation, this group turned to teaching in schools at the primary and secondary levels where they formed a less than dedicated teaching cadre that evidenced discontent. The structure of the intellectual community was bifurcated, with a small minority occupying the better positions at the top and a disgruntled majority working in areas and situations for which they were not really trained and in which they were not really happy.[6]

This situation both aided and hindered CCP plans. The Chinese Communists always regarded the latter group of intellectuals as a potential source of support. They responded to calls for patriotic action and saw in the stability promised by the CCP a chance to improve their positions. Members of the former group were also viewed by the Party as potential supporters, although because of their closer association with centers of Kuomintang power, they regarded them with less enthusiasm.

Yet, at the same time, the Party was and remains suspicious of intellectuals. They frequently have acted independently of Party control, a fact which made discipline difficult. Also, Party leaders correctly perceived intellectuals as members of the bourgeoisie, the very class that was to form the target of the continuing revolution. The CCP had first to heal the rupture within the intellectual community and then enlist their support. But, even if they were successful in both endeavors, the CCP was aware that it had enlisted a force whose revolutionary commitment was open to question. The CCP was forced into an alliance in which each side agreed to cooperate with the other but only with reservations and some doubt.[7]

Chinese communist ideology combined with the historical-cultural and material problems inherited from the pre-1949 era to produce certain tensions as the Party began the process of constructing a new educational system. Clearly one of the first priorities involved correcting the abuses and inequalities of scale and distribution of educational opportunity that had emerged prior to the Liberation. In the same way, it was necessary for the Party to establish a formula by which they could take advantage of foreign experience and expertise while at the same time consolidating independent control of a system that produced graduates who could better meet planned needs for economic and physical development. The challenge for the Party was to raise up a sufficient number of literate, skilled, and secularized graduates while at the same time providing expansion in all sectors of the economy so that they could be absorbed in ways that were useful to the nation and meaningful to the graduates themselves. This was the easy task! The ideology of the Chinese Revolution also required the inculcation of values, attitudes, and behavior patterns that were consonant with the demands of China's emerging socialist society. In addressing this complex problem the Party had to create a system of economic and political organizations that would support the movement toward socialism. They also had to create an educational establishment that would draw ideological sustenance from the general political system and which would in turn support the values upon which the system was based. The problem was one of providing management for a system of revolutionary education in a revolutionary society.

To say this is to say that the CCP needed either to resolve certain tensions or at the very least to allow the tensions to continue and thereby spark progress. For example, should the system of management emphasize centralized or decentralized patterns of control? How much authority should devolve to local units and how much should be retained by the bureaucratic structure? Similarly, given the need for inculcation of political-moral values by relating the classroom experience to the larger problems of life, what should be the role of the professional educator in relation to the role of the individual who lacks technical capacity but who is more than acceptable on political grounds? Should political education be treated as another subject or should it be integrated into the curriculum in more dramatic ways involving participation in labor and other face-to-face contacts with the concrete world? Finally, the management structure had to deal with the tension between Chinese and non-Chinese inputs into the educational process. The values of the system cause the Chinese to look outward to the world of proletarian internationalism: all of the experience of the socialist world should in theory at least have the potential for adaptation to Chinese conditions. But, as is witnessed by events since 1958 when the People's Republic broke with the Soviet Union, this may not always be the case. There is tension between the need for assistance on the one hand and the possibility that such contact may breed dependence or worse on the other.

The evolution of education policies in China since 1949 reflects different approaches and strategies for dealing with basic problems and for resolving tensions that are produced by the interaction of ideological imperatives with the reality of China's physical and human conditions. Despite certain attempts to interpret it so, educational development has not been linear. It has reflected a willingness to improvise, to depart from established norms, to experiment, and to return to earlier modes and practices. In the Chinese view education develops and changes as the course of the revolution changes. Let us see how this is so.

1949-1952: Reconstruction, Rehabilitation, and Reform

On October 1, 1949, with the proclamation of the People's Republic, the Chinese Communist Party turned its attention to reforming the school system. The Ministry of Education, which was immediately established, worked with different regional authorities to coordinate emerging plans and programs at all levels. Later, in November 1952, a separate Ministry of Higher Education was established to devote exclusive attention to problems connected with university reform, then under way.

Of most immediate importance was the problem of imparting a modicum of unity to a national school system. The CCP inherited a system of education that had evolved in rather piecemeal fashion since the turn of the century. Although some unity had been achieved when the Kuomintang established its control in the early 1930s, the new government regarded it as less than suitable to its needs. Nonetheless, to minimize social dislocation they decided to accept the basic structure and to concentrate on changing its spirit, its philosophy, and its methodology.[8]

Although generalization is difficult, the system inherited from the pre-1949 era consisted of six years of primary school, which were frequently subdivided into four years of lower primary and two years of upper primary education. Students then moved, usually by competitive examination, into three years of lower middle school and then, again by competitive examination, into three years of upper middle school. Thus, the secondary component, comprising six years, combined with the primary school experience to embrace twelve years of so-called basic education. Secondary education was further divided into different tracks. General secondary schools prepared students for college or university admission. However, there were also a number of specialized secondary institutions that trained students to be teachers at the lower middle-school and primary-school levels or offered vocational training. The latter institutions produced technicians, clerical personnel, soil and conservation officials, and the like. Unlike the general secondary schools, the specialized units of the secondary system offered terminal degrees and their graduates usually entered the labor force immediately after graduation. In 1949-1950 there reportedly were 24,391,000 students enrolled in China's primary schools while secondary school enrollment at all levels was recorded at 10,039,000.[9]

Students from the general secondary schools "examined into" institutions of higher learning, which reportedly numbered 200 and were located mainly in the major urban centers of the eastern seaboard. Peking, with 50 such institutions, clearly continued to be the cultural capital of the nation. Statistics indicate that in 1949-1950 there were some 117,000 students in the higher education system.[10] Clearly the organization inherited by the CCP was of small scale and could serve only a fraction of the more than 130 million young people of school age.[11]

During the years of the Civil War and the Anti-Japanese War, the Chinese Communists had themselves developed a rudimentary system of education at all levels which they implemented in the areas under their control, especially in Yenan, where they had established their major base. After some experimentation they had decided that a regular and academically oriented system such as that extant in Kuomintang-held areas was not suited to the needs of China's general population. Accordingly they implemented a system of "people-managed, government-assisted" (min-pan kung-chu) schools, also called the "Yenan Model," in which the courses were greatly shortened. A typical primary course might last from one to three years, middle school was compressed to a maximum of two years, and the university component might last from one to two years.[12]
Apart from the reduced length of the curriculum, the CCP felt the major advantage of the min-pan schools to lie in their ability to adapt their courses of study to local conditions and matters of local importance. Courses were specific, addressed to the solution of local wartime problems, stressed immediate

solutions, and did not reflect the assumption that education was designed to provide a means of upward mobility. Best of all, the min-pan schools were self-supporting in that they were financed by local villages, towns, counties, and the students themselves — who from time to time paid small fees. While no reliable figures exist to provide an idea of the number of students enrolled in the min-pan schools, the number was certainly less than those enrolled in the regular system.[13]

In 1949 the Chinese defined their problem as one of integrating these two different models to form a national educational system. But the task involved much more than the simple adjustment and merger of two different "model" systems. It is important to note that what was attempted was the combination of two different approaches to education, which differed in their assumptions concerning the nature of the educational process, its purposes, and to whom it should be available. The attempted merger thus exacerbated problems that already existed and heightened the potential for political conflict within the leadership. This conflict has resurfaced from time to time and become known as the "struggle between the proletarian and revisionist lines in education." The Great Proletarian Cultural Revolution and the struggle against the Gang of Four are rooted in part in the lack of consensus that characterized Chinese Communist educational circles as early as 1949.

If in 1949 the deeper implications of the proposed merger were perceived by China's leaders, they preferred to avoid overt disagreement. The official document of reform, issued on August 10, 1951, adopted the structure inherited from the Nationalists with but slight modification. The major difference as explained at the time was that the system would now be open to all and especially to the workers and peasants, that it would be "rational," producing skilled personnel in planned ways, that it would provide opportunities for political education, and that it would permit flexibility of method in achieving desired goals. In practice this meant that local units were free to innovate in the utilization of texts and teaching materials as long as they followed certain general lines for overall development. More important, it also meant that the Yenan tradition of Chinese communist education was carried forward by linking to the regular system a series of min-pan institutions, especially in the rural countryside and the factory quarters of the urban areas.[14] The network of min-pan schools embraced different formats. Some were full-time units run by villages, towns, urban districts, and neighborhood committees that were distinguishable from their regular counterparts only by the inferiority of their equipment and the location of their buildings in old temples, homes of the former wealthy, and the like. Other units, however, were locally run spare-time schools which were attended by students at the different levels after completion of their daily production tasks. Thus thirteen- and fourteen-year-olds received in their spare time basic instruction and in some cases even secondary education. Perhaps most significant was the development of spare-time literacy classes in which members of the older generation received an introduction to the number of characters required for minimum literacy. In effect, min-pan had come to mean both people-run regular education and people-run spare-time education. In theory, a graduate of the min-pan system could transfer over into the regular state-supported system, and an adult who started in a min-pan literacy class could also enter the other components of the system and progress to its highest levels.

However, it was clear that the reforms did in fact produce two tracks: the state-run schools and the embryonic min-pan schools in both spare-time and full-time formats. The "Decision" of August 10, 1951, acknowledged this and cited the need to equalize the availability of educational opportunity throughout the nation. After some discussion of the causes, the document acknowledged that there were not enough places available and announced plans to tackle the problem by reducing the period of primary schooling from six to five years and the period of secondary schooling from six to three or four years, depending upon the geographical area and whether the school was general or specialized. This was intended to open a larger number of places and also to free up resources for allocation to the min-pan component.[15]

In higher education the changes were more dramatic, with a slight if temporary reduction in the total number of colleges and universities. Perhaps of greater significance was a turning away from the liberal arts concept in higher education and the reorganization of existing institutions into specialized units. While the general number of institutions remained about the same or declined slightly in number, China could point to a change in the number of specialized technical and scientific colleges, universities, and institutes. This reform also had the advantage of breaking up traditional centers of academic independence, especially in Peking and Shanghai, by combining their facilities, giving each a different mission, and reassigning teaching staffs.[16]

Reviews of both primary and secondary sources for this period indicate that the reforms did not produce a great deal of public reaction. While some were dismayed when former foreign-run units were closed or consolidated, there did seem to be an impression that the system was working to decent advantage. This is confirmed by steady increases in enrollments and in the number of graduates from all levels of the school system.[17] In fact, on August 21, 1952, a National Administrative Conference on Elementary and Secondary Schools announced that preparations for the introduction of five-year elementary schools that autumn were already well underway and that the system had already been implemented in Peking. The Peking experience was to be used as a model for replication in other areas. The conference also announced a large-scale expansion of China's secondary schools under the shortened curricular format and called for a large increase in the number of primary- and secondary-school teachers. It seemed that the reforms would be carried through and that there would be a meaningful reduction of the difference in educational opportunity and quality between the urban and rural areas.[18] While not announced by the conference, it has become known that at that time approximately 7 percent of the state budget was allocated to education and that a major portion of that amount was earmarked for expansion of primary and secondary education.[19] But then a change occurred.

1953-55: "Statism" and the Schools

In June 1953 a Second National Education Work Conference was convened in Peking. The result of the conference was an apparent turning away from the spirit of the earlier reforms which seemed to commit the state to encouraging complete education for all, and toward a system whose structure reflected a desire to maintain a moderate scale and the insurance of quality. For example, the report of the conference made no mention of the shortened programs in the primary and secondary schools, commented on establishing a general educational policy, and noted that the agenda had included studying ways and means of regulating primary schools, studying enrollment in primary and middle schools, and formulating plans for "making a success of a selected number of middle schools and normal schools."[20]

Forces set in motion at the Second National Education Work Conference received concrete expression five months later in November 1953 when the Government Administrative Council (the cabinet) issued a "Directive Concerning the Reorganization of Primary and Secondary Education." This directive explicitly rejected the idea of implementing the five-year primary system on a national scale on grounds that enforcement efforts to date had shown the idea to be unsuitable. Officials were directed to stop implementation forthwith. The directive quelled for a time at least the idea of pressing for the beginnings of a system of universal education. It also called for an increase in the growth of urban schools relative to those in the rural areas in light of the more rapid increases in population and industrialization in China's cities. Rural areas were apparently denied means to increase educational opportunities at state expense on grounds that it was more efficient to allocate such resources to the urban sector where graduates could more readily be incorporated into the labor force. The perception of a reduction of state interest in universal education from the lowest to the highest levels receives added credence when it is noted that the directive also ordered that primary-school graduates in both urban and rural areas should be told not to expect to enter middle school after graduation. They were to be encouraged to take up productive labor. The ideal had changed from one of making education available in some form for all who wanted it to producing a rather smaller number of better-educated individuals who could be of maximum utility in China's quest for modernization.

Two other elements of the directive are also illustrative of the new priorities. First, the government affirmed that the central task of the schools was to teach and that all activities that interfered with or detracted from this central mission were to be curtailed or eliminated. This was an obvious reference to the programs of political study, labor participation by regular school students, and the program of field trips to learn about revolutionary history and the like that had become an integral aspect of the life of all students at all levels. Political and ideological training, or what would be called values education in the United States, was relegated to the position of just another subject, albeit an important one. Put differently, while political and moral training continued to constitute a vital portion of the daily curriculum in the primary and secondary schools, its teaching became increasingly confined to the school building. Moral and political education became intellectualized subjects for classroom study rather than disciplines learned by direct participation in programs linked to other sectors of society such as the workers and peasants. Whether intentionally or not, the CCP leadership had effectively slipped the ideological mooring that mandated definition of the schools as but one component of the larger educational environment and had come to focus on the classroom as the major source of educational and revolutionizing experience.

Linked with this element of the November 1953 decision was the assertion that from the promulgation of the document onward, city and county governments should take full financial responsibility for the operation of regular primary schools. Thus, in a sense, the central government was turning all responsibility for local schools over to the agencies of local government. The effect of this was to increase local governments' control over education by making them more than mere conduits of money. They now had greater if not complete control over the resources they generated to keep the schools operating.[21]

A concomitant of this apparent movement toward professionalization, routinization of the classroom experience, and concern with tapping a smaller number of brighter students for advanced study was a marked increase in the role of Soviet pedagogy and Soviet curricular materials in the schools, especially at the newly formed scientific and technical institutes. Between the years 1949 and 1955, approximately 2,000 titles were translated into Chinese. During the year 1953, which is most relevant to the present discussion, 277 textbooks were translated into Chinese and made available for use by Chinese students. Once again the postsecondary level took the lion's share. While impossible to verify, reports indicate that between 1950 and 1957 the Chinese printed and distributed some 190 million copies of 12,400 books.[22] It is tempting to argue from these figures that the period 1953-55 saw a wholesale adoption of Soviet methods and techniques into China's schools and that the Chinese system evolved into a carbon copy of its Soviet counterpart. While there may be some truth in this charge, and it has been voiced by a large number of Chinese at different times in recent years, it is possible to overstate the case. A more practical interpretation is probably that after 1953, the Chinese realized that they could not afford a system of universal education and that it would be necessary to make some compromise with previously stated goals. At the same time, they wished to take maximum advantage of the experience of non-Chinese nations and they quite naturally turned to that of the leader of the socialist world, the Soviet Union. By that time, the Soviet system itself had come to place political-moral education in a more bookish context and the Chinese simply followed suit.

Little is known about the state of China's colleges, universities, and higher technical institutions during this period except that their enrollments continued to grow and that their curriculums reflected an increasingly Soviet flavor. The effect of the November 1953 decision was to reduce the number of students who entered the middle-school system and who could therefore compete for admission to higher educational institutions. But although the number of places available for postsecondary students was still smaller than even the reduced number of applicants after 1953, the effect was not to reduce enrollments in that area.[23] Rather, competition intensified and the emphasis for college students as for their counterparts at the lower levels was on academic performance. Labor participation and other more direct patterns of engagement were not cast aside but rather were replaced by more traditional, intellectually oriented approaches to moral-political education.

The events of 1953 did not, however, spell the end of the concepts of min-pan and spare-time education. On the contrary, as the state withdrew increasing amounts of support for primary and secondary schools, the leaders were forced to acknowledge a continuing need to educate those who were not in the government-supported track.[24] The logic of this dilemma brought the leadership right back to the min-pan format that had arisen from the Yenan tradition. Although this movement did not assume full force until 1955 and just after, the seeds were sown in 1953 and the problem was fixed for Party leaders to confront as conditions developed. Previously min-pan schools were creatures of local production units that sought to meet certain specific needs. After 1949 these needs tended to even out as China moved into a period of peaceful development. Thus there appeared an element of continuity among the people-run schools throughout the country. And even had they been so inclined, and they were not, the leadership could not have risked cutting off the min-pan movement since it was often the only opportunity available for education in large areas of the country. Therefore, with the beginning of retrenchment in 1953 and its formalization in 1955, the government was forced once again to devote attention to the min-pan schools. However, in light of the 1953 reforms, these units had acquired a reputation as being less than adequate and not at all the same as the so-called regular system. Because of this, the government had to take steps to address the "two-track" theory and regularize the min-pan schools. This occurred after 1955, indicating that the period between 1953 and 1955 represents not so much a rejection of the concept of locally supported education but rather a period in which it was placed to the side while the leadership dealt with other problems. However, the tension between the two concepts of education continued to exist and was reflected in subsequent events.

1955-57: Internal Criticism and Response

In 1955 formal approval was given to trends set in motion some two years earlier. On July 22, 1955, Minister of Education Chang Hsi-jo addressed the National People's Congress and announced plans to reduce the budget for education to one-third of the amount spent in 1953 while at the same time preserving its quality. This meant that funds for improvement of existing resources and new capital construction would be concentrated in areas of high population density that had already demonstrated advancement in industrial productivity.[25] Actually, Chang's speech was the ministry's response to an earlier announcement of the priorities of the First Five-Year Plan, which had been revealed on July 5-6. The plan called for increased emphasis to be placed upon upper middle and higher education. Increases in primary-school enrollments were to be restricted, however, to an increase of 18 percent of those that existed in 1952. This was justified because the state needed funds for development in other sectors; educational priorities would have to be readjusted in response to these needs. To take up the slack, the state announced a policy of encouraging people to organize to meet the demand for increased cultural services. There was to be new growth in the min-pan movement.[26]

The 1955 strategy, however, involved several problems of implementation. First, the state placed itself in the position of having to spark the movement to develop local schools. The movement therefore became a part of the "mass line." Second, the min-pan schools were correctly perceived to be inferior to schools supported by the state. Thus it was necessary to address the issue of quality of locally run education. Third was the problem of centralization and decentralization. What should be the role of the state and the Party? Should they encourage the spontaneous development of these units and let them run according to local needs and conditions or should they maintain some element of control over standards and operating procedures?

In December 1955 the Ministry of Education adopted a plan for universalizing compulsory education through utilization of the mass input. The ministry planned to achieve seven-year universal and compulsory education on a national scale. However, different sectors of society were expected to achieve different levels. For example, in larger industrial areas, education was to reach the lower middle-school level. In less-developed but prospering areas, a full primary system was to be achieved. Finally, in the rural countryside, achievement of lower primary education was indicated. The ministry's plan ultimately called for universal education to the lower middle-school level in all medium-sized and industrial cities and for full primary education in all other places by 1967.[27]

The net result of this plan was to reduce the role of the state as a source of funds for educational expansion, but to increase the saliency of its leadership role and that of the Party in the process of overall development. While expenditures dropped, concern mounted, for the plan for universalization could be met only by mass mobilization under CCP supervision and control. Thus, the period 1955 through 1957 saw an increase in the number of institutions at the primary and secondary levels, an increase in the number of students enrolled in such units, and an increase in Party concern with education in the non-state-supported sector.[28]

While the policies of official retrenchment in the state-supported sector and official encouragement of the people-run sector were being implemented, the Chinese Communist Party itself was being forced to acknowledge and respond to certain problems. These extended to all sectors of Party operation but were particularly relevant to schools and universities.

Party actions since 1949 had stirred a tension that had always existed between the CCP and China's students and intellectuals. In consolidating their control, Party cadres had imposed a series of constraints that were resented by older intellectuals and students alike. Consequently, intellectuals were no longer quite so enthusiastic as they had been and there were signs of a slowing down of progress in scientific research and development.

Recognizing this, in January 1956 Chou En-lai announced to the Party that it was necessary to pay particular attention to work among China's intellectuals to better enlist their support. Chou acknowledged that many criticisms were justified, especially those that centered upon the insensitivity, lack of intellectual awareness, and work style of the Party's cadres. Party members, Chou asserted, had alienated many intellectuals by their "commandism" and "bureaucratism." Also, he said, the Party and government must do a better job of assigning intellectuals — graduating college students — to meaningful work posts.[29] In response, in May 1956 an internal Party rectification movement began in which CCP cadres heard criticisms, responded to them, and in theory at least tried to adjust their work styles.

Also in May, China's intellectuals were reminded of their importance in the new society. The head of the Propaganda Department of the Party Central Committee announced that there should be a period of "blooming and contending" within intellectual circles so that the best ideas could emerge, thereby hastening China's progress. "Blooming and contending" was to include ideas on the relationship of the Party to the educational establishment and ideas about the best means of organizing for achieving developmental goals. Intellectuals were being reassured that they did in fact occupy a very important position. However, the response of the community was moderate and confined largely to narrow technical issues. The campaign was an apparent failure.[30]

Then, in February 1957, Mao Tse-tung affirmed the need for "blooming and contending" in a speech before the Supreme State Council. After its limited and edited publication in June and

July, in an essay entitled "On the Correct Handling of Contradictions among the People," educators were encouraged to speak with increasing frankness.

Their indictment was severe. The Party was charged with promoting programs of blind imitation of outmoded and useless Soviet experiences, frustrating the growth of a creative spirit, and imposing a rigid control over the operations of schools and individual departments. Non-Party administrator-intellectuals were seen as powerless figureheads who had no real voice in determining educational policy. While the overwhelming majority of criticisms did not challenge the assumption of the appropriateness of Marxism-Leninism for China, the CCP was called upon to allow authority to devolve back to the individual colleges and universities. The Party could not but react against the "blooming and contending," for its control was severely challenged.

After this "summer of storm," a study conference was convened in Peking to deal with the problem in the capital's universities and colleges. The study conference concluded that despite certain advances in drawing worker and peasant students into the university system, most students were in and of the bourgeoisie; they were of "bad" class origin. Later, similar conclusions were drawn about university faculties and research staffs. Thus, the reason for the "Hundred Flowers" turning into "Poisonous Weeds" was seen to reside in the lack of political awareness of teachers and students. Policies of the past were criticized because it was now clear that they had failed to provide effective political education.

The decision of the study conference produced several remedies. The most important of these was the antirightist campaign in which professors and students analyzed their mistakes to reform their outlooks. A second aspect of the program involved increased efforts to recruit students of worker and peasant origin, while the third involved the mounting of a "campaign to discuss socialist education." As a result of the events of 1956-57, China's colleges and universities turned from traditionally academic pursuits to an increased emphasis on political-moral education. Professors and students became politicized: they were articulating their interests and were objects of a campaign for the remolding of political outlook. Earlier formulations which had relegated political studies to the realm of an academic subject were replaced by a renewed emphasis on specifically political training by direct extra-classroom confrontation with the data of political life.

The period 1955-57 saw a diminution of resources available for state-supported education and an expansion of the role of the Party/government bureaucracy in the non-state-supported sector. It also saw the emergence of an internal critique of political-moral education that led the Party to increase further its control over educational affairs. Finally, as the Party reasserted its hegemony, it did so in a manner that involved the introduction of political criteria and symbols that had been put aside in 1953. The stage was set for the increased politicization of China's schools.

1958-1960: The Great Leap Forward

Early in 1958 China embarked upon a nationwide campaign to increase productivity in all sectors of the economy. This was known as The Great Leap Forward. The Great Leap saw the expansion of communes in the countryside and a marked increase in their economic, social, and political functions. In brief, the Great Leap was an attempt to achieve dramatic improvements in material production by mobilizing every available resource. If there was insufficient mechanization to achieve desired goals, masses of human beings were mobilized to take up the slack. Thus, thousands of people worked alongside mechanical earthmovers to build dikes and irrigation canals, and city dwellers joined peasants in planting and harvesting alongside mechanized farm implements. China was attempting to unify the modern and the nonmodern sectors of the society to achieve new goals, a concept known as "Walking on Two Legs."

The Great Leap Forward was of extreme importance for

Chinese education, for it brought into the open a concept of "revolutionary education" that had received uneven attention since 1949. Also, the Great Leap occurred at a time when education circles had been forced by the "blooming and contending" of the Hundred Flowers Period to reevaluate the relationship between the classroom and the larger society in constructing and operating an educational system. Thus the Party was in a good position to undertake the upcoming changes.

The priorities for the Great Leap Forward in education were set forth in a directive of the State Council issued in September 1958. The plan envisioned that by the end of 1959, student enrollments at all levels would be increased by 45 percent over that of 1957. There was also to be a corresponding increase in the number of schools. It was assumed that the vast majority of the new students would be of worker or peasant origin.[31]

The most interesting feature of the Great Leap plans, however, was that these tremendous increases were to be accomplished not by a massive infusion of state funds but rather by the creation of new schools at all levels that would be financed, supported, and run by local factories and communes. According to the directive, schools that were already in place were to open factories to generate funds for use in expansion, while factories and communes were to finance, support, and operate schools out of their own funds. The min-pan concept had not only been adopted but expanded in unprecedented ways.[32]

The Great Leap both effected innovations in the educational system and reinforced some earlier trends. For example, the full-time state-supported system remained and even expanded; however, students spent more time in productive labor than had previously been the case. Usually, the proceeds of their work reverted to the school so that it could expand its activities. Similarly, the program of spare-time schools was greatly expanded and supported largely by funds garnered from newly tapped local sources in factories, communes, and full-time schools that now had additional sources of income. As in the past, spare-time schools ran the gamut from basic literacy classes to newly established spare-time universities. A new structure introduced in 1958 was the half-time school. The students in these units were employed members of the labor force who attended classes for a portion of each working day. The production unit ran the school and provided necessary staff and facilities.

While the goal and the format of the full-time state-supported schools remained basically the same as before (except for the introduction of a high component of labor participation), the half-time and spare-time schools were more varied in orientation and format. These schools were created by production units and were designed to serve their specific needs. Because such needs varied from place to place, programs also varied. Communes founded agricultural middle schools in which emphasis was placed on raising levels of agricultural technique as well as achieving basic literacy. In factory-run schools, the emphasis was on imparting knowledge to enhance productive techniques. In some cases the Great Leap involved the formation of "red and expert" universities, usually run on a half-time or spare-time basis, in which the level of instruction, while still task-specific, was higher than at locally supervised primary or middle schools.[33]

The Great Leap Forward resulted in an increase in the complexity of China's school system. In addition to a growing number of schools, there were also increasingly varied orientations and formats. Similarly, the movement increased exponentially the quantum of political-moral education to which individual students were exposed. Irrespective of whether the student was engaged in full-time, spare-time, or half-time study, he or she was constantly made aware of the political dimension of China's revolution. The September directive made it clear that education was to serve proletarian politics and be combined with productive labor. Thus there was a reemphasis of the link between the classroom and the larger society, a link that had been allowed to lapse in earlier years. As a result of the Great Leap, Chinese education became politicized on a larger scale than ever before.[34]

A part of the rationale for the Great Leap policies lies, of course, in the economic realm. The state could not afford to underwrite a system of universal education, and economic sense dictated that production units assume the burden. But to understand the movement in all of its ramifications, it is also necessary to turn to the ideology of China's revolution. By making a direct link between education and labor, the regime was attempting to effect a change in the way in which education was perceived by the Chinese masses. It was not to be seen as a step on the ladder of upward mobility. Rather, education was to be regarded as an opportunity that enabled one to make an increased, direct contribution to society. By educating workers and peasants and by having students engage in labor, the government hoped to erase the distinction between mental and manual labor that has plagued Chinese society for more than a thousand years. The Great Leap Forward in education was not only an attempt to educate more people; it was also an attempt to educate them in a different way and for a different and more revolutionary purpose.[35]

Finally, it should not be assumed that the Great Leap reforms in education, despite their emphasis on local units, involved an effective diminution of Party control. While the reforms did cause problems for the education bureaucracy in that they were to "run by themselves," it should not be forgotten that the Great Leap was Party, and therefore government, policy. The reforms were carried out by the Party with a mass-line emphasis, and it was this that was to provide unity and direction in a time of rapid change. Decentralization did not necessarily involve the loss of Party control. On the contrary, as with the tentative reforms in the min-pan schools in 1955, the Great Leap reforms were predicated upon an increase in the role of the CCP in determining all aspects of the operation of local schools.[36]

1961-66: Readjustment and Compromise

However, even the superior organizational and communications capacity of the Chinese Communist Party was inadequate to cope with the major changes in social policy wrought by the

Great Leap. Changed goals, new procedures, and new forms of organization placed a load upon China's administrative structure that soon proved to be too heavy. The Great Leap Forward sputtered to a close, and by 1961 the leadership was moving in different directions. So too was educational policy; between 1961 and 1963, certain dramatic changes occurred.

In 1961-62 a series of meetings was held in which the future of the educational system was discussed. If these meetings were publicized at the time, they received scant or no public attention. In 1963, however, the Ministry of Education announced a number of important changes in the mission, method of operation, teaching methodology, and, by implication, relationship to society of China's primary and middle schools. Education in China had reverted to a pattern that reflected, in part, the priorities discussed in 1953.[37]

Most dramatic was an apparent redirection of educational strategy away from providing some form of basic, highly practical, and intensely political education for large numbers of students, toward provision of "quality education" for a much smaller number of students, who would then enter the postsecondary track. The reforms were defined and implemented in interesting ways.

Quality education was defined as constituting a corpus of basic theoretical knowledge taught in the classroom by instructors who themselves were custodians of the data. The teachers were to focus on development of individual achievement, not group progress. In primary schools, emphasis was to be placed upon the "Three R's," while at the secondary level, advanced mathematics would be joined by programs in science and foreign languages. Promotion was decided according to individual student performance as determined by competitive examination. The new reforms set aside the ideas of group learning through practice that were so emphasized during the Great Leap, in favor of essentially intellectual processes for individual learning. Related to the emphasis on teacher-centered classroom learning was a corresponding decrease in the time allocated for political study and training. Specific limits of between three and five hours per week were set aside for political and extracurricular activities. A rigid, ministry-provided standard curriculum was instituted, and special permission was required from the county or town education office before any deviation from the approved schedule could occur. Thus, the newly emerging system was characterized by more centralization.

The reforms announced in 1963 also called for the upgrading of the position of teachers. In many cases salaries were raised as older teachers received both credit for years of experience and bonuses or equalization raises to compensate for alleged past neglect. Finally, the important role of the teacher in society was emphasized. Younger teachers were admonished to learn from those of their colleagues who enjoyed the benefit of greater experience so that they too could become effective teachers. In fact, the teacher was held up as an object for popular esteem on a scale rare in China since 1949.

Another aspect of the new professionalism was the identification of so-called "key schools" in which the new reforms would initially be implemented. Key schools enjoyed excellent facilities, better-trained teachers, new curricular forms, and, of course, brighter students. After 1963 they were enhanced, which caused them to be reviled during the Cultural Revolution as "little treasure pagodas." In effect, the key schools received the best that China had to offer in terms of staff, facilities, curriculum, able students, and presumable level of instruction. They were the schools that provided the upper levels of the entering university classes.

This was in fact an important aspect of the post-Great Leap Forward program. Under the new mandate there appeared to be a clear emphasis on preparation for entry into the postsecondary track. The stress on science, mathematics, and especially foreign-language training does not suggest that these primary- and middle-school graduates were expected to immediately enter the labor force. On the contrary, it seems clear that the intent was to prepare the students for entry into the highest levels in the most effective ways possible. Thus, after the Great Leap Forward, the relationship between the lower, middle, and higher levels of the system was integrated more closely.

The implications of the new system were far-reaching. First, the new form implied a diminished concern about the half-time, spare-time, and <u>min-pan</u> school formats in favor of almost total emphasis on the formal, full-time, state-supported component. While not all of the more flexible, practical, and politically oriented, locally run schools suddenly ceased operation, without active government/Party encouragement and support, their number declined as did the morale of their students, teachers, and graduates. After the Great Leap, the idea of mass education of any type was seriously qualified in practice.[38]

More important was the <u>de facto</u> downgrading of political education and of the idea that learning is to provide immediate practical result and should therefore be conducted in an atmosphere that reflects social practice, including participation in practical labor. Teacher-centered, book-oriented education displaced the form so prevalent during the Great Leap, which emphasized direct apperception of the materials for learning in a setting of which the teacher was but one part.

This is not to say that political-moral education was neglected or shunted aside. Between 1963 and 1966 there were three major campaigns among China's students: to "Cultivate Revolutionary Successors," to "Learn from the Army," and to develop socialist consciousness by participation in the Socialist Education Movement. Similarly, although the time devoted to political education was reduced in the primary grades, it continued to form an integral aspect of the curriculum at all levels. Finally, participation in campaigns that extended to the whole society, when coupled with even reduced political studies, produced an atmosphere in China's schools that can only be termed political. Politics was and remained a salient issue for teachers and students alike. What did change, however, was the context in which political-moral themes were presented. No longer at the core of the curriculum and no longer enforced by direct participation in activities, political-moral education became just another subject in the ministry-approved curriculum. As had been the case in 1953, the study of politics had become comparatively intellectualized.[39]

Perhaps the most significant aspect of the reforms after the Great Leap was that by 1964, and possibly earlier, China had a two-track system of education. One track was constituted by the state-supported component with the key schools at the center and the other by the remnants of the half-time, spare-time, min-pan system that had been built up since 1958. Graduates from the first track tended to move to the postsecondary level while graduates of the latter track moved directly into the labor force. Of course this situation had obtained before but the existence of two separate tracks with different aims and purposes had always been explicitly denied! Different types of schools had existed, but they were being integrated into one national system. It seemed now that the Party retreated somewhat from that commitment, content to allow the question of tracking to ride while they tackled the larger questions of formulating an educational plan. Indeed, in the eyes of many observers, tracking now seemed to form an integral aspect of that overall plan.[40]

1966: The Great Proletarian Cultural Revolution

It seems apparent that between 1949 and 1966 the Chinese leadership shifted back and forth between two different conceptions of what form of education was best suited to China's emerging goals and priorities. It also seems clear that shifts in education policy were derived from different ideas of proper goals and priorities for continuing the Chinese revolution. Shifts in education policy reflected larger tension rooted in political and ideological questions. By 1966 these larger questions had become major issues of Chinese politics, for individuals had staked their political viability on their commitments to different responses to larger ideological problems. In effect, the debate over whether education should provide basic education for development of a skilled and cultured labor force or whether it should produce experts for technical development was a by-product of the debate over the best way of continuing the Chinese revolution. In spring and summer 1966, the issue was joined in an event known as the Great Proletarian Cultural Revolution, which necessarily had great effect upon the educational system.

In August 1966 the Party Central Committee issued a decision closing the schools at all levels, enjoined students to go into the streets to make revolution, and prescribed certain changes in the structure of the system to make it conform to a new vision of revolutionary society. In their new role as Red Guards, students (mainly from middle schools and colleges and universities) took to the streets to destroy the "Four Olds" (old ideas, customs, habits, and culture). Schools at all levels were closed as students accused teachers and administrators of supporting a system that had turned away from the revolutionizing values of the Great Leap Forward. The new system prescribed by the Central Committee was but one issue in a larger debate involving both individual political power and conflicting definitions of the proper course of China's revolution.[41]

The major indictment of the system as it had developed since 1961 was that it tended to produce a class of individuals who had theoretical knowledge but no ability to apply that theory to practice. Also, graduates were characterized as elitist in that they felt their theoretical knowledge put them above the masses of workers and peasants. In sum, while the system may have produced experts, it did not provide students with a clear set of value-referents to give them direction and motivation. They were studying for selfish purposes of individual advancement and not to make a contribution to the continuing revolution. The remedy required restructuring of the system and a change in pedagogical technique in order to place the younger generation on the proper revolutionary track. However, it is difficult to discuss this restructuring in a systematic way because it was never implemented fully; the larger question of who held the reins of political power was never totally resolved. The tension that assumed crisis proportions in 1966 continued to exist and, as will be seen, continues to exist at present.

The major contours of the Cultural Revolution reforms can be summarized as follows. First, the period of schooling at all levels was reduced. The twelve-year primary-secondary cycle was reduced to ten years, with five years of primary school, three years of lower middle school, and two years of upper middle school. However, although the time of instruction was reduced nationally, the form of the reduced format varied somewhat from place to place. Thus, there were integrated ten-year schools, six-year primary schools, four-year integrated middle schools, and a variety of other formats as well. A related effect of the restructuring of the system was a blurring of the distinction between its different levels. No longer was there a line of clear demarcation between the primary, secondary, and postsecondary units.

A second and more important dimension of the new program was expressed in the concept of "Open-Door Education." This meant that the schools and the educational process were to be integrated into the total social environment and that the resources of the whole environment were to be mobilized to support the classroom experience. In practice this involved many far-reaching changes. But it should be noted that all of the changes had precedent in earlier CCP experience.

The practice of "Open-Door Education" involved the following types of changes. First was a marked increase in the importance of moral-political education. No longer a bookish undertaking, politics was to be placed at the core of the curriculum. This meant a great deal of emphasis on the study of the works of Mao Tse-tung and other classics of Marxism-Leninism. More important, political-moral education was linked once again to direct participation in productive labor. Students were to learn by active and direct confrontation with the accumulated experience of the Chinese Revolution as expressed in productive labor and close relations with the workers and peasants.[42] To facilitate this, the system of school management was decentralized, with communes, production brigades, and production teams taking control of all units in the countryside, and factories assuming control of urban units. A new form of school administration, the revolutionary committee, was prescribed. It brought together representatives of the workers and peasants, revolutionary cadres, and teachers and students in a so-called

"Three in One Combination" that would ensure a truly mass, nonprofessional input into local school administration. For the same purpose, examination criteria for movement between the different levels of the system were abolished and students were permitted to advance essentially on the basis of political fitness as evaluated by the revolutionary committee (the masses). As criteria for promotion within the system changed, so too did criteria for admission to the system. Children of workers and peasants were admitted almost automatically to the schools in an attempt to make the student population more reflective of the class composition of Chinese society generally.

The perceived advantages of the new system were similar to those articulated in 1955 and 1958. Local control under centralized guidance would save state resources which could be allocated to other areas, it would provide for maximum flexibility of form and content in response to local requirements, and most important of all, it would make it possible to reinforce the ideological-moral imperative that education was to be undertaken to make a maximum contribution to social-political development. Again echoing the words of the 1950s, education was not to provide social mobility; rather, it was to produce individuals who had skills and were able and willing to apply them where and when they were needed, irrespective of individual desires and preferences.

The movement for flexibility of form and content also provided the rationale for changes in the curriculum as well as in teaching methodology. The Cultural Revolution reforms saw a recrudescence of half-time and spare-time units designed to meet the needs of particular production units. Similarly, in the former "regular schools," apart from the increase in time spent in political education and productive labor, there was a reduction in the amount of time allocated for instruction in the more traditional areas of science, mathematics, and foreign language. Because no one form of primary- or middle-school curriculum was ever implemented on a national basis — there were several approved models — it is impossible to generalize about shifts in the allocation of time to teaching of different subjects. However, all sources indicate that even when these subjects were taught, it was imperative that they be related in some form to concrete reality. Thus, students of physics worked in electrical plants and students in rural schools measured and surveyed the fields of the brigade or team.

A final thread that ran through all of the reforms was the idea of "collectiveness" in all areas of school operation. Decisions regarding curriculum were to be the consensus of the collective leadership of the revolutionary committee, as were decisions concerning admission and graduation. Collectiveness was also of crucial importance in the classroom life of each student. Students and teachers were to discuss subjects together in an attempt to bring the whole group to a certain point of knowledge more or less simultaneously. The concept of testing and grading was altered to provide for the teacher posing certain questions which would be discussed together by the students, who then evaluated the level of the whole group and assigned a pass or fail accordingly. If a student failed, the whole group was to exert itself to provide remedial assistance. Individual achievement in theory ceased to characterize the educational process.

The Cultural Revolution reforms hit China's colleges and universities with particular force, for it was at the postsecondary level that heterodox modes of thinking and practice were considered to be most apparent. China's middle and primary schools were reopened in 1967 and 1968 but the universities did not open their doors once again until 1970, and then only on a limited basis. The postsecondary curriculum was shortened from four or five to three or four years, depending upon the institution, and the revolutionary committee became the leading body of each unit. But the most significant change involved the composition of the student body and the teaching staff. Students could no longer proceed directly from upper middle school to a college or university. They were required first to "undergo tempering" on farms or in factories for at least three years before admission could be granted. Also, it was not the university that determined who would be admitted but the "masses" in the production unit who decided essentially upon political grounds whether or not the candidate would make best use of the higher education experience. Local units decided, based upon the conduct of the applicant in the environment of production, whether he or she sought education for the correct ideological reasons or was more concerned with individual fame. The new admission system was tied to the program of "rustication" in which middle-school and primary-school graduates were sent directly to the countryside to work — in theory, for life. By the end of 1975 some 12 million students were reported to have been relocated in different areas of the country.

University teaching staffs were also changed by the addition of workers, peasants, and members of Mao Tse-tung Thought Propaganda Teams who supervised the curriculum of political education. The effect of this practice was to reduce greatly the student/teacher ratio in most colleges and universities and thereby to ensure that the political dimension of higher education not be slighted.

What has been described above is a statement of goals and priorities rather than a complete system of national reform. The implementation was uneven because the central authority of the Party and government did not show consensus or total commitment to specific programs. Individuals who were the target of Cultural Revolution reforms continued to have influence in the educational area and many of the policies simply did not work out in practice or in relation to developmental goals.

For example, in 1973 it was decided to reinstitute examination for university enrollment as a means of placing students. Later it was felt necessary to offer remedial assistance to students who scored poorly on these so-called placement tests. At first, remedial work was counted as part of the regular curriculum but later such work was defined as remedial and not to be counted toward graduation. Similarly, in the primary and middle schools, there developed a renewed concern with standards. If examinations were to be reinstituted, then the lower levels had to take this into account in their own planning and operation. There were also references to problems with the rustication program. Many youth simply did not want to leave family and friends for life in the countryside. What was the use of studying if they were marked for a life of agriculture or factory labor? Finally, the teaching and administrative staffs of the schools had lost, as a result of the Cultural Revolution, any clear sense of what their mission was. Because there were conflicting pressures and demands, they often chose the path of least resistance and did not exercise leadership. That this situation could develop in the decade following 1966 is a function of the internal politics of the Chinese Communist Party. There were those in the Party who, in response to the Cultural Revolution, were willing to resolve the tension by constructing a new synthesis that would embrace elements of both of the apparently contradictory views of what Chinese society should be. But this group did not possess political power adequate to translate its preferences into policy. At the same time, there was a group within the central leadership that had achieved power during the Cultural Revolution and who hoped to enhance and consolidate that power by its continuation. They too lacked control of political resources sufficient to dominate the system. Because of this, between 1966 and 1976 Chinese education reflected the political tensions that characterized Chinese society, and elements of two different models of education existed side by side — to the confusion of the foreign observer and indeed to the confusion of the citizens of China. It was only after the death of Mao Tse-tung in September 1976, and the subsequent overthrow of the Gang of Four in October, that one side was able to predominate over the other. This made possible the establishment of a new political coalition, fragile though it may be, and also facilitated the formulation of stable political-economic policies. Most important for our purposes, it also became possible to establish a coherent education policy.

Our delegation visited China just over one year after the death of Mao and the repudiation of the Gang of Four. At the time of our visit, the new line on education was just emerging and we were therefore unable to describe and analyze it fully. In the following chapters each member of the delegation has recorded his or her impressions of the current education scene in the specific areas that we determined to be most important for understanding the emerging system. Our treatment is neither exhaustive nor conclusive. It is not intended to be. We hope that these impressions will convey an understanding that the values of China's social system provide the CCP leadership with an array of approaches and strategies to be used in conducting education and that social change continues to be an enduring moral imperative. We interpret what we have seen not as a turning away from the values of revolution but rather as an effort to achieve a new synthesis of the tensions engendered by the needs for economic development in a context of revolutionary social change.

Notes

1. Mao Tse-tung, "On Contradiction," "On Practice," in Selected Works of Mao Tse-tung (Peking, 1965), vol. I, pp. 295-310, 311-47.
2. Mao Tse-tung, "The Chinese Revolution and the Chinese Communist Party," ibid., vol. II, pp. 305-34.
3. Y. C. Wang, Chinese Intellectuals and the West, 1862-1949 (Chapel Hill, 1966), especially pp. 99-145.
4. Ibid.
5. Confirmation of this impression is seen in ibid., pp. 164-90.
6. Ibid., p. 377.
7. For an authoritative theoretical statement about the role of intellectuals in the Chinese Revolution, see "Analysis of the Classes in Chinese Society," in Selected Works of Mao Tse-tung.
8. Jen-min chiao-yü [People's Education], November 1951.
9. State Statistical Bureau, Ten Great Years (Peking, 1960).
10. Ibid.
11. Precise, reliable figures are difficult to attain. This figure assumes China's population at the time to be around 450 million. Thirty percent of this figure yields 135 million school-age youth. Thirty percent was selected because of references by Chinese leaders to the effect that about that percentage of the total population required schooling. For example, see Jen-min chiao-yü, November 1951.
12. Michael Lindsay et al., Notes on Educational Problems in Communist China 1941-1947 (New York, 1950), pp. 37-44.
13. Ibid.
14. Jen-min chiao-yü, November 1951.
15. Ibid.
16. Leo Orleans, Professional Manpower and Education in Communist China (Washington, D.C., 1961), pp. 57-61.

17. Enrollments changed as follows between 1950 and 1952:

	Primary	Secondary	Postsecondary
1950	24,391,000	1,268,000	117,000
1951	28,924,000	1,825,000	137,000
1952	43,154,000	3,126,000	153,000

Source: State Statistical Bureau, Ten Great Years (Peking, 1960).

18. "New Elementary School System to Be Applied China Over," New China News Agency (NCNA), Peking, August 22, 1952, translated in Survey of China Mainland Press (SCMP), no. 401 (August 24, 1952), p. 22.
19. Orleans, Manpower and Education, pp. 14-16.
20. "Second National Educational Work Conference Convened in Peking," NCNA (Peking), June 5, 1953, translated in SCMP, no. 584 (June 16, 1953), p. 22. For a fuller discussion of these issues see Joel Glassman, "Centralized Planning, Decentralized Administration: Community Control in Chinese Communist Education" (Paper presented at the 30th Internal Congress of Human Sciences in Asia and North Africa, 30th Internal Orientalist Congress, August 3-8, 1976, Mexico City).
21. "GAC Directive Concerning the Reorganization and Improvement of Primary School Education," NCNA (Peking), December 14, 1953, translated in SCMP, no. 726 (January 13, 1954), p. 23. Also see Glassman, "Centralized Planning."
22. Orleans, Manpower and Education, pp. 12, 117.
23. In 1953 postsecondary enrollments increased from 153,000 to 191,000. See Ten Great Years.
24. For example, between 1951 and the end of 1954, the percentage of all students of higher education who enrolled in the spare-time track increased from 0.3 to 4.6, or from 400 students to 9,700 students. See ibid.
25. Jen-min jih-pao [People s Daily], July 25, 1955.
26. Eighth National Congress of the Communist Party of China (Peking, 1956), vol. 1, pp. 229-59.
27. Glassman, "Centralized Planning," pp. 20-22.
28. By the end of 1957, primary and secondary enrollments had increased as follows:

	Primary	Secondary
1952	43,154,000	3,126,000
1957	63,464,000	7,059,000

Source: State Statistical Bureau, Ten Great Years (Peking, 1960).

29. Chou En-lai, "On the Question of Intellectuals," NCNA, January 29, 1956, in Current Background, no. 376.
30. The following discussion borrows from Theodore E. H. Chen, Thought

Reform of the Chinese Intellectuals (Hong Kong, 1960), chapters 13-18.

31. Stewart Fraser, Chinese Communist Education: Records of the First Decade (Nashville, 1965), p. 50.

32. Lu Ting-yi, "Education Must Be Combined with Productive Labor" (Peking, 1958).

33. George P. Jan, "Mass Education in the Chinese Communes," in Stewart Fraser, ed., Education and Communism in China (London, 1971), pp. 127-45; and Munemitsu Abe, "Sparetime Education in Communist China: A General Survey," in ibid., pp. 239-53.

34. See Lu Tung-yi, "Education."

35. Ibid.

36. By the end of 1959, enrollments in the regular system had reached the following levels:

primary	86,400,000
secondary	8,520,000
postsecondary	660,000

Enrollments in the "nonregular" system were as follows:

primary	26,000,000
secondary	5,000,000
postsecondary	150,000
literacy classes	40,000,000

Source: State Statistical Bureau, Ten Great Years (Peking, 1960).

37. "1963 Temporary Work Regulations for Full-time Middle and Primary Schools," translation and commentary by Susan Shirk, The China Quarterly, July-September 1973.

38. For example, by 1962 the number of agricultural middle schools had dropped from 22,600 enrolling 2,030,000 students to 3,715 enrolling 266,000 students. 1968 Yearbook on Chinese Communism (Taipei, 1968), p. 194 (quoted in Donald J. Munro, "Egalitarian Ideal and Educational Fact in Communist China," in John Lindbeck, ed., China: Management of a Revolutionary Society [Seattle, 1971], p. 277).

The results of the reforms, if not the figures, are confirmed in "Chronology of the Two-Road Struggle on the Educational Front in the Past Seventeen Years," Chiao-yü ke-ming [Revolutionary Education], May 6, 1967, translated in Peter Seybolt, ed., Revolutionary Education in China: Documents and Commentary (White Plains, N.Y., 1973), pp. 5-79.

39. Interviews conducted by the author in Hong Kong, June 1968-July 1969.

40. Ibid.

41. "Decision of the Central Committee of the Chinese Communist Party concerning the Great Proletarian August 12 Cultural Revolution (August 8, 1966)," Peking Review vol. 9, no. 33 (1966).

42. Ibid.

ORGANIZATION AND STRUCTURE

Thomas C. Schmidt

Commissioner of Education, Rhode Island

Although the purpose of this chapter is to outline the organizational structure of education in the People's Republic of China, several problems complicate the task. First, the provinces, cities, communes, and production brigades we visited during our eighteen days in China are located in areas that are among China's most developed. None of these communes can honestly be called a "rural" commune, for instance; "suburban" is a more accurate term. This fact alone makes it difficult to describe the structure of Chinese educational organization on a countrywide basis. But our task is further complicated by the second fact: our hosts, while willing to discuss the overall form of organization of the education system, were unable to be specific about the nature of the relationship between the system's various components. An official in Nanking stated quite frankly that such information is not made public, and officials at different levels in Kwantung Province were either unclear or uninformed about the specific structure and methods prevailing in other provinces. A third factor is that recent years have witnessed a number of contradictions in China's concept of education; these contradictions have created such turmoil and confusion that it is still difficult for Chinese educators to adjust. Ever since the outbreak of the Cultural Revolution in mid-1966, the education bureaucracy has been buffeted by forces emanating from opposite ends of China's political spectrum. Before it ended, the Cultural Revolution managed to turn around a number of policies that had been standard before 1966. Subsequently, since 1971-72, bureaucrats have been called upon to reimplement policies and procedures that bear striking similarities to the pre-1966 pattern. It is only now, with the "smashing of the Gang of Four" in late 1976, that educators are able to assume a period of relative stability in educational policies. Bureaucratic leaders at all levels explained to us that regularized procedures and practices were still emerging. For these reasons our hosts were unable to answer our questions in definite terms. Nevertheless an outline did emerge.

The Party

Our briefings and speeches of welcome repeatedly indicated that the organizational structure of education is nested within the Chinese Communist Party, that bureaucratic decisions in the sphere of education reflect the policy preferences of the Party, and that these decisions are manifested in the "Party line" at determined times. Furthermore, the education system and its organization exist to serve the people, and it is the Party that defines the interests of the people in terms of "building socialism." As Westerners, we were tempted to assume, because of our own liberal experiences, that bureaucratic latitude for individual innovation and change was nonexistent in China. It is still our impression that although a certain tension does exist at times between the demands of the central authorities and the preferences of provincial and local units, lower-level units can at best modify or adapt only slightly the priorities set by central authorities. Impetus for major change comes from the top; there is room at the bottom for minor adjustments only.

If ideas are adopted and supported within the Party, then organizations at the lower levels are obligated to implement and carry out these policies. In this regard, Western bureaucrats and the organizations they manage have extraordinary autonomy compared to their colleagues in China. Whereas individuals in the West frequently contradict established policy or conventional directors (especially when they can muster support from the political or bureaucratic structure), that approach is rare in China. There are exceptions. Powerful counterthrusts to established policy or current leaders are not unknown, as the events of the Cultural Revolution and the controversy engendered by the Gang of Four illustrate. However, this section of our report attempts to describe the usual process, the typical structures of organization as they are emerging in China today.

The Educational Process

The ordered structure of China's educational system is reinforced by a standardization of processes. The budget, for example, is developed in basically similar ways for every school, college, prefecture, and province. Common methods are used to make decisions in other areas as well. We were impressed by the Chinese practice of decision making by rules and standardized criteria, within a system that is more structured than any in the United States.

In informal discussions with cadres along our route we learned that in China, as elsewhere, bureaucrats tend to fall into informal groupings based upon length of tenure, length of Party membership, common provincial or regional origin, and shared experiences in the development of China's revolution. While the cadres we met were generally more inclined to discuss their current activities than their past experiences, they did identify themselves in certain ways such as "anti-Japanese war cadres," "civil war cadres," "land reform cadres," and the like. When we asked if anyone ever relied upon friendship or special relationships to get things done through the "old boy network" we were told this was not the way in "new China." Other apparently less-guarded conversations drew the admission that some Chinese still on occasion try to get favors for themselves or for their institutions by "going in the back door." It is indeed possible that many of China's schools do in fact base their organizational structure upon the informality and simplicity of the "old boy" system, even though it is publicly frowned upon. Even given these opportunities for unofficial leeway within the system, however, the reader of this report would not be wrong to assume that China possesses an educational structure more formal, more ordered, and less open to informal influences than that of the typical bureaucracy in the United States. Let us now turn to an examination of the structure of the central education bureaucracy.

Bureaucratic Structure and Organization: The Center

The highest level of organization is the national Ministry of Education located in Peking. The ministry reports directly to the State Council, an organization encompassing the various ministries of the Chinese government. A Peking-based cadre told us, however, that the Ministry of Education more frequently communicates with the State Council through the Planning Commission, a body consisting of representatives of the various ministries and which organizes their activities into a coherent plan or program so that their functions do not overlap.

In matters such as budget deliberation, the ministry's proposed budget — derived initially from sub-provincial-level recommendations — is reviewed by the State Council's planning commission staff. Cadres with whom we spoke in Peking and Nanking indicated that there is a certain amount of alteration, bargaining, and adjudication involved in this relationship, but that ministry proposals are not usually altered in a dramatic manner. The national budget, to continue the example, is of course set by the State Council with education as one part. When the State Council makes gross manpower training decisions for the country, surveying, for instance, how many and what types of engineers China's industry needs, it transmits these goals to the Ministry of Education so that it can train enough engineers to meet this need. After gross manpower decisions are made, the Ministry of Education, in consultation with the staff of the State Planning Commission and at times in meetings with the full State Council itself, prepares a series of educational budgets and directives that are handed down to pro-

Organization and Structure   43

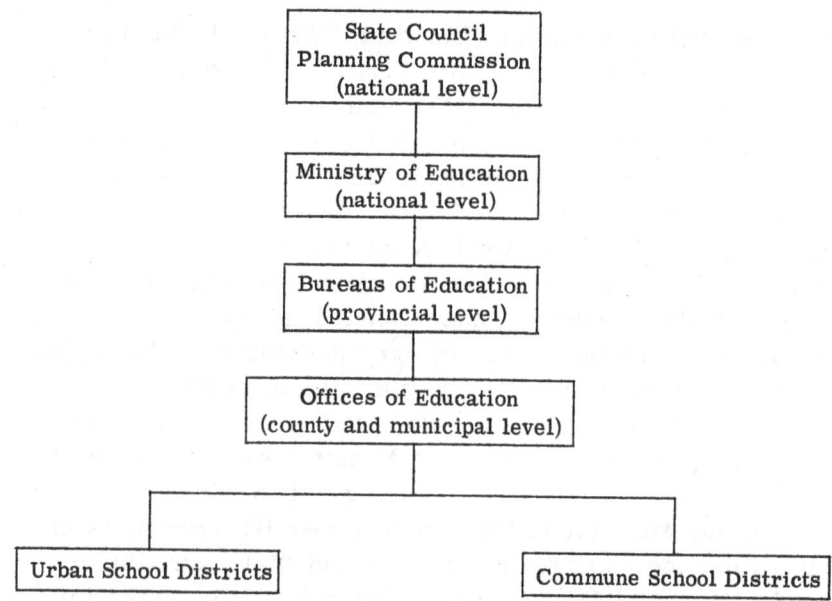

Figure 1. General organization of education in the People's Republic of China.

vincial bureaus for administration.

The general organization of education in China from the State Council to the neighborhood schools is shown in Figure 1.

We were surprised to find that the organization of the Ministry of Education is characterized by a rather small number of subdivisions, called offices, and by a staff that is small in comparison to similar organizations in the United States. Interestingly, no ministry cadre with whom we spoke could or would provide the exact number of ministry personnel, but several agreed that the staff numbered between 400 and 450.

The Ministry of Education in Peking was reinstituted just a few months before our arrival in China and was reported to be immersed in organizing itself even during our stay. The Minister of Education, Liu Hsi-yao, told us that the ministry had ceased to function in the Cultural Revolution era, during which time its operations had been carried on in a limited manner by the Science and Education Commission of the State Council, and to a greater degree by local authorities acting on their own without central supervision. Liu said, "We are trying to improve that. We now have a unified, nationwide plan which all local, municipal, and provincial organizations must carry out." Minister Liu continued by saying that China's schools will no longer have to follow "double leadership." According to our delegation's principal guide, Mr. Hu, the same group of individuals who functioned under the Science and Education Commission as the "leading group" for education now constitute the core of China's reemerging educational leadership.

Mr. Hu was also the source of our information on the organizational structure of the offices within the ministry. After breakfast one morning, as our "soft-bed" train was approaching Nanking, Mr. Hu reported that the Ministry had six major offices, and a seventh was just beginning to take shape. All are headed by the Minister of Education, whose background is in organization and supervision of heavy industry. Mr. Hu answered with a qualified "yes" when we asked if Minister Liu had been chosen because his background will enable him to upgrade the quality of China's scientific and technological education. But when we followed this with a question as to whether or not Minister Liu had brought with him his staff associates from his earlier job as China's Minister of Industries, Mr. Hu replied with a friendly but unqualified "No, things are not done that way in new China."

The six major offices over which the Minister presides are divided along functional lines. The Office of Foreign Affairs deals with visiting delegations and with exchange visits by Chinese nationals to foreign countries for study and conferences. Since it is the ministry's Foreign Affairs Office that had responsibility for arranging and supervising our itinerary, we naturally gained some familiarity with its operation and organization. The office is organized according to a formula that balances geography with language. For example, our immediate hosts were attached to the North American and English group of the office. However, one of our escorts had done temporary duty in English-speaking Africa. Members of our delegation were impressed both by the level of competence in English exhibited by the personnel and by their general familiarity with American customs. While we did not determine the size of the office staff itself, we ventured it to be between 60 and 65 by virtue of the fact that the Ministry has six offices and 400 employees.

The <u>Planning Office</u> is in charge of the development of long-range plans, including manpower training projections which become an integral part of budget decisions. We were able to gather very little information concerning this office, but several impressions did emerge. For example, we felt that this office provides the ministry's most direct linkage with the State Council and the Council's Planning Commission. We were even led to believe that there was some overlap between the staff of this office and the staff of the Planning Commission, although we were never able to verify this to our satisfaction. Similarly, we were not able to develop a sense of the number of staff personnel who perform overlapping functions, but we were assured that extremely close contact was maintained. Subsequent conversations with provincial bureaucrats led us to conclude that most of the planning work of the ministry is essentially short-term, with projections made for about two to three years into the future. However, announcements made following our return to the United States concerning China's long-range development plans, especially in the areas of science and technology, may result in some change.

The <u>Worker and Peasant Education Office</u> is similar to adult or continuing education offices in the U.S. education system. This office sets goals and priorities for education of those Chinese who are beyond the ages of attending traditional schools or universities. Again on the basis of conversations conducted at the provincial and local levels, we were able to infer that this office is assuming increasing importance as China extends adult and continuing education as part of the strategy of "walking on two legs." Universities and colleges in China's various provinces are responsible for providing short courses, correspondence courses, and in-service training for individuals who for various reasons are not attending regular institutions of secondary or postsecondary learning. Cadres at all levels noted the importance of such courses, and as we learned from Madame Fang Fei, deputy leader of the Kiangsu Province education bureau, for example, significant resources are being allocated to programs of this type. Continuing the process of inference, we concluded that the Worker and Peasant Office has responsibility for leadership in developing curricula for these programs, for ensuring that basic standards are met, and generally for coordinating the efforts of the provincial and municipal educational institutions in conformity with national targets. In fact, if plans for the development and expansion of July 21 Factory Schools and May 7 Agricultural People's Universities are met, this office of the ministry may well come into contact with by far the largest segment of China's population engaged in academic study.

The Mid-level Technical Specialties Office deals with technical schooling, exclusive of university-level technical training. We were unable to gather any significant information about the role and mission of this department.

The Higher Education Office, as the name implies, is in charge of university education. The duties of this office extend to virtually all aspects of university supervision and leadership, from approval of curriculum to development of textbooks and approval of university teaching and research personnel. The Higher Education Office was said to work closely with the Planning Office in exchanging information that bears upon the feasibility of plans being developed at the Planning Office, although the greater part of its effort is directed toward solution of current problems of university operation.

The functions of the Elementary-Secondary Education Office once again are explained by its title. This office reviews the

Organization and Structure 47

development of different aspects of secondary and primary education including text preparation, approval of personnel assignments, approval of curriculum plans, and the like. Several cadres at the municipal and provincial levels told us that they were making monthly trips to Peking to speak with members of the office in connection with the development of a system of unified texts.

During our automobile ride from Yangchou to Nanking, Kiangsu Province education officials told us more details about the seventh office which was then being created within the Ministry of Education. Called the <u>Liaison Office</u>, the function of this unit will be to coordinate its work with that of other ministries which Minister of Education Liu Hsi-yao said will also be sponsoring educational institutions of their own (e.g., a school of mining under the Ministry of Industries, a ballet and opera school under the Ministry of Culture). Our delegation visited one such school, the Nanking Power School, an upper middle school that trains electrical technicians and skilled workers and which is led by the Ministry of Petrochemicals.

The Liaison Office has been designed to coordinate the educational efforts of each of the ministries and to provide a central reference point for the development of such activities. A cadre from the Ministry of Education explained to us that the creation of this office is a direct outgrowth of the new policy of emphasizing scientific and technological education. Officials from both Peking and Nanking thought that such a body is necessary to keep the Ministry of Education abreast of the needs and requirements of the other more technically oriented ministries and also to enable the Ministry of Education to coordinate these activities. Another purpose of the Liaison Office is of a more symbolic nature: to remind all bureaucrats of the importance of upgrading scientific and technical education according to rational and ordered procedures. We were not able to uncover any information regarding the composition of the staff of the office or its real position within the Ministry of Education

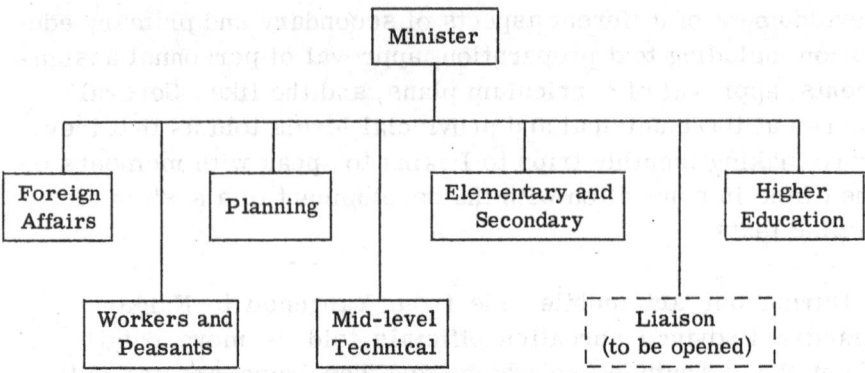

Figure 2. The Ministry of Education, Peking.

and relative to other ministries. However, we do feel justified in concluding that the Liaison Office or an equivalent body will become increasingly important as China continues to implement its new educational plans.

Provincial Structures

The Ministry of Education, the State Council, and the Planning Commission of the State Council are known collectively as "the center" by bureaucrats at the provincial and lower levels of the educational structure. Beneath "the center" at the provincial level is the education bureau, which until the Fifth National People's Congress in March 1978 functioned as part of the overall structure of provincial-level government known as the provincial revolutionary committee. Although revolutionary committees were abolished at the 1978 conference and replaced by regular supervisory organs at the provincial level, education bureaus continue to form a part of the provincial governmental structure.

The provincial education bureau carries out the functions of initial planning and control. It is responsible for screening and forwarding requests, reports, and general information from the universities, colleges, and school districts of the provinces to the central ministry. The bureau also transmits to "the center" information and requests from the prefectures, districts, municipalities, and counties that constitute the non-education-related elements within a province. Finally, the education bureau in most cases is the sole interface between "the center" and the lower district and commune levels, although this is not true in the case of special schools and institutions run by ministries other than the Ministry of Education.

During the automobile trip from Yangchow to Nanking, our delegation learned that the provincial bureau plays a major role in coordinating the education-related efforts of other governmental and nongovernmental organs. For example, the bureau staff schedules visits by local health agencies to schools during which students receive examinations, innoculations, and special health education. In the same way, staff members arrange labor assignments for local schools and schedule special projects for members of the Youth League, Red Guards, and Little Red Soldiers. Thus, extracurricular and "enrichment" activities receive official supervision and support.

Figure 3 shows the provincial structure as we pieced it together after interviews with cadres in Nanking, Shanghai, and Canton. Despite repeated checks with separate individuals, it was impossible to tell if all functions noted on the chart are in

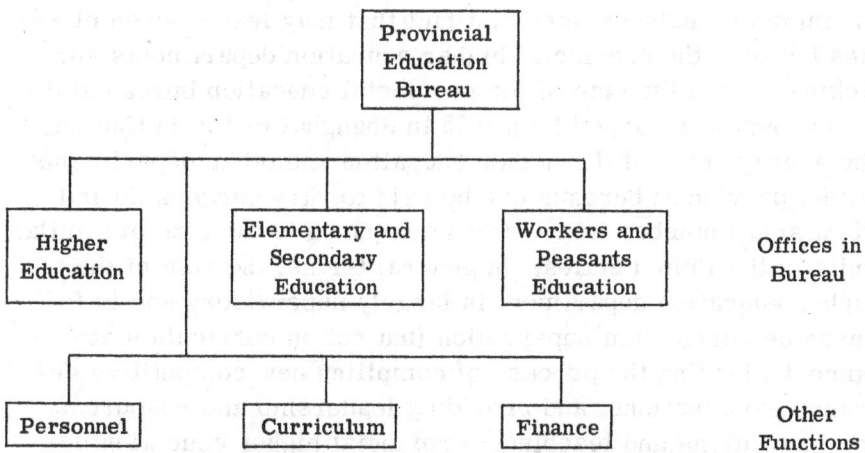

Figure 3. Provincial bureau functions.

fact performed by departments with that particular designation. Therefore, Figure 3 is best seen as a chart of provincial-level functions rather than as a chart with an accurate list of the names of all of the different organizational units in any particular province.

The higher education department has responsibility for overseeing the administration of all the institutions of higher learning in the province. Although the role of the department may be less direct in the case of institutions connected with other ministries, department staff members are familiar with the problems and operation of all educational units in their province. The higher education department seems to play a more significant role in the planning activities of the Education Bureau than any other department with the possible exception of the finance department. The relative importance of this department may stem from the impression that higher education is more politicized than secondary and elementary schools, and therefore more deserving of attention by "the center." Whatever the reason, the higher education department seems also to have closer links with Peking than other departments within the provincial bureau. During the time of our visit, Chinese educators began a series of meetings to develop a unified curriculum and textbook series, a fact that may lead to even closer ties between the provincial higher education departments and Peking. Since the size of the provincial education bureau staffs we encountered ranged from 125 in Shanghai to 150 in Canton, the average size of the higher education and other departments within provincial bureaus can be said to vary between 20 and 25, a small number indeed when compared to the size of similar units in the United States. In general terms, the role of the higher education department is largely supervisory and is focused on curriculum supervision (but not on curriculum development), leading the process of compiling new competitive entrance examinations, and providing leadership and resources for innovations and teaching. Provincial higher education departments hold regular meetings in which the aims and purposes of new programs are discussed and teachers and school administrators make suggestions and offer models which are examined and criticized. These meetings also report on experiences with different kinds of materials and experimental approaches to education. In this way the higher education department both introduces new programs and at the same time maintains a degree of control over their content. During our visit, educators from different units held meetings several times each week.

The elementary-secondary education department of the provincial education bureau emerged as a rather broadly gauged organization with roots that extend deep into provinces. Not only does the department work with primary and secondary schools, but it also has direct linkages with the Communist Youth League organization as well as the Red Guards at the secondary level and the Little Red Soldiers in the primary schools. This reinforces a previously held view that this department leads the primary and secondary education process while it integrates the activities of extracurricular organizations into a system that supports traditional instruction-oriented activities. In Nanking, cadres reported that the department has good lines of communication throughout the Kiangsu Province and that the information it provides is usually of very high quality. The department also supervises the maintenance and evaluation of the curriculum at the primary and secondary level by gathering information and enforcing regulations concerning the amount of time spent in instruction in different components of the curriculum during the school year. Our impression was that much of the department's time is spent in monitoring performance of primary and secondary schools and in reporting the results of these observations to Peking, via the provincial education bureau.

The workers and peasants education department is a provincial extension of the department located within the central ministry in Peking. Its function is to upgrade the educational levels of individuals who for various reasons have ceased to participate in the formal educational process. At the same time, it enables this segment of the population to gain a foundation of theoretical knowledge to complement practical ability gained in years of work practice. Theoretically, this department will help workers and peasants to acquire the ability to understand new skills and techniques and to apply these in work situations. This concept is known in China as "walking on two legs," or utilizing more than one available resource in order to realize a policy objective. Accordingly, the worker and peasant department undertakes to design, implement, and supervise courses in continuing adult education. These, we were told, range from courses in basic literacy to middle-level courses in agricultural techniques such as sericulture and animal husbandry and courses designed to produce qualified industrial technicians. Members of our delegation were impressed by the diversity and range of these courses and programs and by the ability of the department to "tap" the resources of nearby universities to find instructors to teach the courses. We were not able to develop a sense of how many students were enrolled in continuing education programs or to assess their impact. Similarly, we were not told whether participation in these programs was viewed by students as a step on the ladder of upward mobility within the system. It was clear, though, that the cadres with whom we spoke had little idea of the real effect of these courses, although they all agreed that the idea was sound in principle. Thus the department has two missions: The first is to upgrade general cultural levels for those workers and peasants who are judged to be below the educational standard. Its second mission is to take those who have achieved some degree of general knowledge and enhance it by practical training in particular areas. In discharging these tasks, the department appears to make good use of the resources offered by the faculties of institutions within the province. Finally, since the department is engaged in carrying out what has been announced as a high-priority policy, its status, at least in formal terms, seemed to us to be fairly high.

Thus far we have discussed those units of the education bureau that deal directly with the schools, colleges, and universities in terms of a general mission. Each unit mentioned has responsibility for a particular type of education. Our discussions also touched on other departments whose functions cut across the different levels of educational institutions and whose staffs view the provincial educational system in a somewhat larger perspective.

The personnel department, for example, has responsibility for the assignment of staff to schools based on the needs of those institutions and a comprehensive plan for manpower development. In fact, every teacher is an employee of the provincial government and, in a sense, of the central government as well. Therefore, each teacher is posted to a particular assignment for a specific reason, which usually, we were told, relates to his or her special abilities or experience. Transfers between schools at the same level, and particularly transfers from one level to another level, require the approval of the provincial education bureau through its personnel department. If, for instance, an upper middle school requires a teacher of physics, the school administration has to forward a request to the personnel department, whose staff undertakes the necessary search and decides who should receive the assignment. Teaching staff are not free to change jobs as they wish. Rather, they must wait to be engaged by local units whose request has been approved by provincial authorities. In making teacher and administrative assignments, such matters as proximity to family, the need for a father or mother to be near home, and similar matters are taken into consideration, but decisions are based ultimately on the actual needs of the system.

Our discussions, particularly at Nanking Normal College, also revealed that the personnel department is involved in student enrollment. For example, we learned that in line with the new emphasis on scientific and technical education, it has become necessary to assess the specializations of teaching and research staff at the colleges and universities within Kiangsu Province. The personnel department, in conjunction with the higher education department, has the task of identifying qualified personnel and making the transfers and additions necessary to carry out the new policy priorities. Presumably, although we were not told this in specific terms, the department acts in the same way with respect to the development of new staff for primary and secondary schools. Thus, the personnel department has an interface with the three mission-specific units of the provincial bureaucracy.

So too does the <u>curriculum department</u>. During our visit, we were informed that each of China's provinces was in the process of developing a standard curriculum for use within the province. Since we were also told in Peking about the development of a national curriculum, we assumed that there will be little basic variation once the process is complete. Our discussions revealed that curriculum development involves a great deal of communication both from below and within the central ministry. Teachers in various subject areas meet regularly to discuss goals and standards. Reports are then made to the curriculum department, whose representatives then travel to Peking for participation in additional meetings designed to produce a standard curriculum. We were led by officials from Shanghai and Peking to believe that this process of consultation is very much confined to "experts" and that the emphasis is on substantive improvement in the teaching of basic intellectual skills.
We also learned that the structure of local school administration facilitates this process. Each of the schools we visited has a group, called the "teaching research group" or the "educational transformation group," whose mission is to evaluate and revise approaches to the teaching of different subjects. In every case, it appeared that the members of these groups are professional educators rather than political functionaries. These groups meet on a regular basis to consider the needs of curriculum development and seem to provide the link between the local schools, colleges and universities, and the provincial education bureau. Our impression was that the system is well developed and that communication is both frequent and effective, at least in the urban areas we visited.

The finance department, as the title implies, oversees fiscal aspects of school administration. It bears primary responsibility for the preparation of budgets as well as for their implementation and, as we learned, its staff works closely with the units at the basic levels. Local schools prepare initial budgets and are required to justify each item. These tentative budgets are reviewed by the finance department and, we were told, some adjustments are usually made. When a school's budget is approved by the province, it is forwarded to the Ministry of Education in a package request where it receives final consideration. If cuts are made in a province's education budget while being approved in Peking, the provincial bureau can either distribute the reduction equally among all its schools or fully meet certain schools' budgets while cutting back severely on others. In the same way, the finance department coordinates funds for supplies and capital construction. Unfortunately, budget figures and amounts allocated for different purposes such as capital construction fall into the category of information which the Chinese do not wish to make public and were therefore unwilling to discuss with us. Thus, provincial-level administrative organization is both lean and function-specific with some units directed toward particular kinds of schools and others organized to coordinate the activities and address the problems of the whole provincial system.

County-Level Organization

The organization of education at the county level reflects the simplicity of organization both nationally and provincially. At the time of our visit, the county seat was the location of a revolutionary committee or leading administrative organ for county governance. A constituent part of the revolutionary committee was the county education office, headed by a "chief."

The county education office provides for the fulfillment of five functions. The administration and politics section, we learned, has basic control of the activities of all schools within

56   China's Schools in Flux

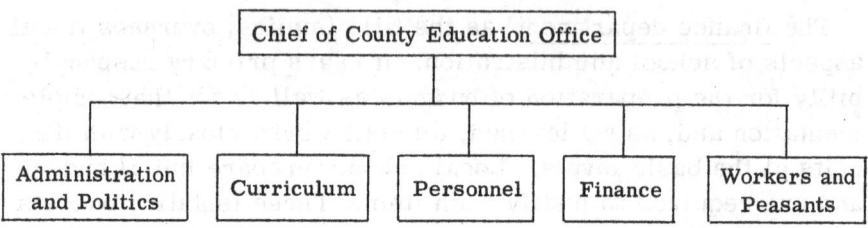

Figure 4. County functions.

a county. It is administered by the chief of the education office, who is also a ranking member of the county committee of the Party. Regarding the size of the staffs of local offices, our conversations led us to the tentative conclusion that they are usually quite small, perhaps staffed by only two or three persons. In effect, all other units of the county education bureaucracy report to the administration and politics section of the county education office.

As at the provincial level, a curriculum section exists whose primary purpose during the time of our visit was defined as participation in the development of a new standard curriculum. This unit exercises the latitude, built into the system, for choosing examples that closely reflect local conditions and circumstances for inclusion in textual materials. It appeared that the county-level curriculum section functions as the source of educational examples which are forwarded to higher levels where they are sifted and winnowed in a nationwide effort to develop materials with universal application. Prior to the introduction of new policies in 1977, the curriculum section had developed, approved, and adapted textbooks to keep them in line both with local conditions and with prevailing political currents.

The personnel section at the county level is responsible for assignment of teaching staff within the different schools and also allocates the number of student openings for various levels and subject areas. Based on their perception of the capacity of the local schools to absorb different numbers of students and also in accord with manpower training objectives emanating from above, the personnel section assigns quotas of students to different types of education at different levels of schools within the county.

The finance section largely mirrors the functions of the finance department at the provincial level. As described to us, the finance section is concerned with the allocation of funds for capital development and preparation and administration of budgets. Finally, the workers and peasants education section, as at the national and provincial level, deals with what corresponds in our own system to adult and continuing education.

We left China with a strong feeling that administration at the local level is relatively less well differentiated and not as sophisticated as organs at the higher levels, presumably because local officials have little power to effect change. At this level we began to encounter educators who were generalists rather than specialists and whose quality of formal training was not nearly as high as at levels above. Also, it seemed clear to us that at the county level and below, school administration refers essentially to the implementation of policies formulated at the higher levels. There seemed to us to be very little opportunity for county officials to influence policy beyond making minor, very "safe" amendments.

Local Organization: Within Cities and Communes

Our delegation did not have an opportunity to discuss educational administration and structure at the district level within one of China's urban areas. Similarly, although we had somewhat better luck in our discussions at the three communes we visited, where our hosts were anxious to discuss the topic, these communes were all located too close to large cities to be called "rural." Our information on education structure at this level is therefore limited and should not be used to generalize either to the situation as it exists within a city or on a rural commune.

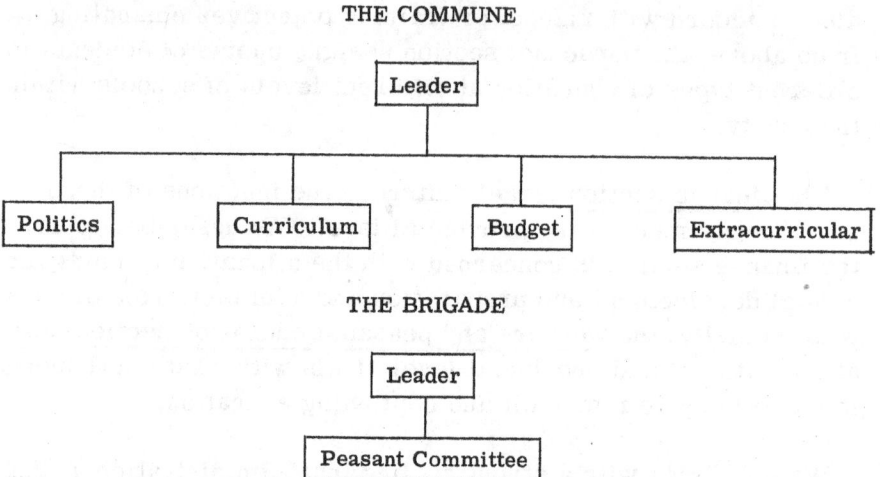

Figure 5. Local education: commune and brigade educational functions.

At the commune level, educational organization is tied even more closely to Party organization than it is at the higher levels. The commune organization administers its schools with the budget provided by the province, which receives its funds according to a national plan for education. Individual communes are encouraged to add a portion of their own funds to the school budget, thus making it possible for the unit to exceed national norms. All the communes we visited were relatively prosperous and in every case commune leaders were proud to tell us that the commune membership had agreed to exceed the norm by diverting additional resources to the education budget. In the one case in which we received information concerning the amount spent for education, we learned that only 3 percent of the total education budget of a commune near Shanghai was derived from its own funds. This figure is essentially meaningless, however, since we were not told the total budget.

Each commune we visited had its own education office. The one near Shanghai is led by seven members, three of whom are responsible for finance and budgeting and one of whom is responsible for overall administration. This latter is also a vice-chairman of the commune's revolutionary committee and a leading member of the commune Party organization. The remaining members of the education office at the commune level divide responsibility for extracurricular activities, political education, curriculum development, and physical training. Few leaders at the commune level have formal training as educators. All have had a minimum of schooling and have demonstrated a commitment to educational work. Beyond this, however, all those we met were clearly amateurs.

This amateurism is most apparent at the level of the production brigade, which falls just below the commune on the organization chart and is the basic unit of accounting in China's countryside. Our experience indicated that it is unusual for a brigade to have more than one or two primary schools. We learned that the general form of brigade education organization is to have one elected, full-time person to oversee the operation and administration of the brigade's schools. This person is assisted by a part-time committee of brigade members who are also elected by the brigade membership. In all cases our delegation witnessed, brigade education officials were strictly nonprofessional educators. For this reason if for no other, China's practice of allowing only minor variations in educational methodology at the local level seems appropriate and wise.

Our delegation reached two interesting conclusions about educational organization in China. First, although the Chinese system remains decentralized to a point (it is governed primarily at the provincial level), China is not taking full advantage of this potential for flexibility and variation. With twenty-nine separate laboratories in which to conduct education experiments, the overwhelming urge is toward standardization. With effort and courage the Chinese could organize an educational system that reinforces local initiative and recognizes the value of a diversity of educational ideas. Our second conclusion is that the function of each level of the system is basically to control that which is below and to be controlled by that which is above. This results in what seems to be an efficient system of resource allocation appropriate to the needs of developing China.

DECISION MAKING

Frank B. Brouillet

Superintendent of Instruction and
President of the State Board of Education, Washington State

Our examination of decision making in the Chinese educational system was both rewarding and frustrating. Our hosts often seemed flattered by our interest in how their system works, but our questions inevitably moved into areas that lie outside the realm of open discussion in the People's Republic. Sometimes we received frank and informative replies. Yet, on other occasions, particularly when we requested specific information on the budget or on the relationship between Party and non-Party members of the bureaucracy, queries were either ignored, answered with a generalization about mass democracy or collective leadership, or directly refused. Thus, while we were able to learn a good deal about the organization of education, we were less fortunate in collecting information about how the system works.

These difficulties were compounded by the complexity of the educational establishment in that enormous country. As we heard at every stop, China is a large, poor, and developing nation with special needs and problems, especially in education. While none of us would disagree with this assessment of China's situation, we all felt a need to qualify it. It is more accurate to say that China is unevenly developed, with pockets of modernity in the urban centers — especially those of the eastern seaboard. As one moves outward to the suburbs and presumably to the rural areas as well, the quality of facilities, the level of teacher training, and the resources available for education show a relative decrease. As a result, we noted that the Chinese in effect run several different educational establishments.

These variations occur within a context of scale that is staggering. The population of China exceeds 800 million — one-quarter of the world's population. Of this number, almost 200 million are in school and a larger number still is of school age. This corresponds to about 217 million inhabitants of the United States of whom approximately 45 million are enrolled in the kindergarten through twelfth grade system.

The visitor cannot but be impressed by the extensive structure and the large number of different programs that have evolved to meet the demands of this complex situation. At the top is the Ministry of Education. This bureaucracy provides general direction and policy formation for the regular school system. We saw that as one moves down the structure, additional administrative levels become involved and overlap. The line between central, provincial, and local bureaucracies is not always distinct.

We learned that provincial bureaus of education supervise all of the schools of each province. They also directly administer middle schools, specialized institutions, and different types of higher education units. Three municipal bureaus (Peking, Shanghai, and Tientsin) are directly responsible to the Ministry of Education while other municipalities, which report to the education bureau of the province in which they are located, run their own nurseries, kindergartens, primary schools, middle schools, teacher-training institutions, and even universities. Neighborhood committees administer and operate elementary and middle schools and are under the supervision of higher levels of administration. At the lowest level, production teams under the control of communes operate primary schools.

In addition to this large and complex regular school system, a significant number of other educational institutions and programs are available to the people of China. We visited and heard about technical schools run by various ministries (with the cooperation of the Ministry of Education), factory-run schools, and countless numbers of classes aimed at bringing adults to a minimum standard of literacy. We noted with approval that many of these courses and programs are ad hoc in nature and have evolved in response to the perceived needs and desires of leaders and people.

How then is this vast educational system controlled and administered? As we have seen, the system is both large and complex. Traditional and nontraditional programs operate at all levels of Chinese society. Undoubtedly, some consistency and direction is essential if there is to be a functioning educational operation.

We found that it is not as easy to respond to this question as it was to make the observations that led to its formulation. We cannot claim to have grasped the patterns of information flow through different loci of bureaucratic power that taken together constitute the decision-making process. However, we did learn something of the way in which Chinese educators describe and discuss their system with foreign counterparts, and we were able to identify certain key concepts that seem to inform the process of leadership. Finally, we were able to gather certain impressions concerning the latitude and leeway that different units of the system possess in relation to those standing elsewhere in the bureaucratic hierarchy. And so, we hazard a number of observations and tentative generalizations on the operation of China's educational establishment.

The Theory of Decision Making: The Chinese View

Before our departure many of us had encountered certain terms that the Chinese use to describe their own politics. However, it was not until the end of our journey, in Canton, that we finally received an explanation of what these terms meant to our counterparts. In each of the cities we visited we arranged to meet with local administrators and teachers for an informal question-and-answer session. Usually these conferences were scheduled in lieu of the afternoon rest, a fact that may attest to the real desire of the Chinese to respond to our quest for information and also to learn from us. In any case, we had decided that afternoon to focus our efforts on determining the relationship between Party-member educators and non-Party bureaucrats. What, we asked, were the limits on a Party official's authority, and conversely, how far could non-Party members and ordinary citizens go in articulating preferences for the practice of education? We also pressed the question of the proportion of constituents of such leading bodies as revolutionary committees and members of provincial and municipal educational bureaus who were Party members in relation to the number who were not Party members, and what roles each type of official played.

After some twenty minutes of questioning, the responses became increasingly succinct. Our hosts clearly felt that we were seeking to identify a Party dictatorship. Finally, after an exchange of glances, one of our interpreters who was attached to the External Affairs Department of the Ministry of Education and who had been with us since our arrival in China proceeded to deliver a short lecture on the nature of China's political system. The burden of his polite but monitory remarks was as follows:

It was clear — and understandable — he said, that we had not yet comprehended the essence of China's political process. To accomplish this it was essential that we understand the concepts of the mass line, democratic centralism, and collective leadership.

In China, we were told, application of the mass line was Chairman Mao's method for developing a form of leadership that did not base itself upon the power of an elite group of Party members but rather converted that power into authority by eliciting the support of the masses. Working Party members — cadres — are to convince the masses (non-Party members) that the Party is the best representative of their interests. Put differently, the mass-line style of leadership enables the Party to gain legitimacy by persuading the masses that its plans and programs indeed serve their interests better than alternative modes. It is also necessary to demonstrate these benefits to the masses in actual practice.

Our interpreter then explained that this process involved a number of regularized and well-established methods of procedure. The cadres, he said, become involved with and work closely with the masses in all areas of endeavor. In this way, individual Party members are able to discover and understand what different segments of the population view as being most important in society. This knowledge is collected and then passed on to the higher levels of the Party organization in the course of Party meetings held in the work environment. Thus the most senior member of the Party in the Ministry of Education can keep informed about what non-Party teachers and administrators at the lower levels are thinking and feeling about a range of important questions.

At the "higher levels" knowledge of the views of the masses is assessed and analyzed in relation to the preferences of the Party about what should be done. We were told that Party desires are often partially modified to better encompass mass preferences. Once this occurs, information is sent back down through the Party apparatus in the form of Party positions on different issues. The masses are then convinced to accept these "new" directions, the policies are implemented, and their success enhances the legitimacy of Party leadership. Our interpreter stressed, with many approving nods from those few Chinese who could follow his comments (they were made in English), that this is an ongoing, continuous process. Utilization of this technique allows the Party to anticipate the views and desires of the populace and to maintain a leadership position where it can direct and lead those wishes.

In addition to establishing the preeminence of the Party's leadership, the mass-line style is said to allow the Party to minimize the utilization of coercive methods. Our interpreter proudly informed us — again with the approval of his colleagues — that the more the populace becomes involved in this process, the greater their influence with the leadership and control over the Party. In fact, he believed that the masses were deeply involved in the process and that the masses did exert control over the Party.

He continued by informing us that the mass line is not only an important link between the Party and the masses but also between the higher levels of the Party and the cadres at the basic levels. This, he said, is how the higher levels provide leadership and control over their own workers. In other words, just as local Party members learn about the thoughts and feelings of the masses, so too do upper-level Party members learn about the thoughts and feelings of their colleagues at the lower levels. Basic-level Party members exert influence and control over the higher levels and have inputs into policy formulation. Our interpreter felt that he had a significant role to play in this process, and all of us thought that he seemed to believe what he was saying.

We were also informed of a self-correcting device in this method of operation. Under continuing questioning, our informant admitted that the Party had at different times lost that close relationship with the masses that is required to make the mass-line style of leadership work. He cited the period prior to the Cultural Revolution and the internal Party turmoil engendered by the Gang of Four as examples of this. However, he also pointed to the concepts of criticism and self-criticism as antidotes to this problem. He told us that in their weekly meetings Party members critiqued themselves and each other on how well they were doing in developing and maintaining mass relations in their respective units. It was clear that he regarded criticism and self-criticism and the need to deliver concrete benefits as an important insurance against the development of Party elitism. He then continued his lecture with a discussion of democratic centralism.

We were already aware of apparent contradictions in much Chinese communist theory, and the concept of democratic centralism was for us no exception. Yet it was clear to us from the remarks of our interpreter and the supporting comments of his colleagues that the Chinese see these two theories as mutually supportive. They described the combination of the two terms as "democracy under centralized guidance" and pointed to the Constitution of the Chinese Communist Party. We later looked up the relevant passage, which states:

> The whole Party must observe democratic-centralist discipline: the individual is subordinate to the organization, the minority is subordinate to the majority, the lower level is subordinate to the higher level, and the entire Party is subordinate to the Central Committee (Article 8).

In fact, we later found that the Party constitution makes several references to a type of democratic process. "Delegates to Party congresses and members of Party committees at all levels should be elected by secret ballot after democratic consultation...." When pressed on the matter of elections, our hosts admitted that candidates were elected from a list that had been approved by higher levels of the Party, a fact that in our view qualified the democratic nature of the process. Our Chinese hosts, however, said that this was not the case because of the operation of the mass line and criticism and self-criticism. They impressed us with their certainty that these elements of the system ensure that the best people are nominated and eventually chosen to fill positions.

Another component of democracy in democratic centralism, according to our interpreter, is seen in the practice of Party leaders at each level reporting to the entire membership of each level. At these meetings, he said, Party leaders inform the membership about the activities of the Party unit, summarize experiences, announce new tasks and problems, and request ideas for improvement of the unit's performance. Again, our host seemed to feel that these sessions were extremely valuable as a means of keeping informed on upcoming problems. He also felt that the information shared was valuable because of its completeness and generally high quality. When we asked whether or not there was a chance for questions in these sessions or if disagreement was ever expressed about the appropriateness of a particular course of action, we were told that such practices varied in frequency. If a policy was being announced, then discussion focused on the best means of implementing it, and disagreement might be expressed in one or another of these points. However, if it was announced that the topic was "open for discussion," then differing points of view were put with force and assertiveness.

A third aspect of democratic centralism as presented in this brief lecture centered upon the idea of internal Party criticism. Party members, we were told, have the right to criticize Party organizations and their leaders at all levels. If necessary, individual members may even bypass the leaders of their own units and approach leaders higher up in the hierarchy. In trying to determine the frequency of this kind of action and the limits upon it, we were told that such actions were rare because this was seldom necessary. In a later conversation we learned that such skipping of steps did occur during the Cultural Revolution but that that period represented a special case. In the session itself we were told that virtually anything was open for criticism except the Marxist-Leninist underpinnings of the system itself.

We were deeply impressed by the apparent sincerity with which these ideas were expressed. It was clear to us that these Party members and officials seemed truly to believe in the efficacy of the procedures they described. Certainly we received an impression that the Party is aware of the need to promote democracy within its own ranks. Whether or not one part of the democratic-centralism process is more strongly emphasized than the other has varied at times during the history of the People's Republic. In times of stress and difficulty there appears to have been more emphasis on the centralist aspects of democratic-centralist theory, while during times of stability the emphasis has been placed upon the democratic aspect of the theory.

Our informant concluded his remarks with a commentary on the third important base for decision making in China, the principle of collective leadership. He noted that while democratic centralism deals with the interaction and relations among units, collective leadership refers to the interaction and relations among members within a specific unit. This means that the

Party believes that many heads are better than one and that decisions are likely to be more appropriate if they are based upon the experience and the wisdom of the collective. All important decisions are to be the consensus of the whole body of members of a specific unit. In essence, the principle of collective leadership, as it was explained to us, means that Party members within a unit meet, discuss, and arrive at a consensual decision. The decision is then transmitted to the other members of the unit. Since Party members are familiar with the Party line, they will mold any decisions around Party ideology and the Party line, as received from higher levels.

Obviously what we received in this ten-minute disquisition on CCP leadership style represented a statement of the process in ideal terms. We of course have no way of knowing how the actual reality reflects or diverges from these stated ideals and it is fair to say that none of us was at all convinced that all worked as we were told. However, we must note that our informant, who had clearly explained this to non-Chinese before, and his colleagues who obviously agreed with and supported him were extremely clear about the meaning of the terminology, that they obviously believed in what they were saying, and further, that they were deeply committed to working within the context of the decision-making system. In sum, whether we accept it or not seemed to us to be quite beside the point. The Chinese education leaders that we met in Canton seem to accept it completely. We feel that we must be aware of and respect these feelings in subsequent dealings with the Chinese Party bureaucracy.

The Structure of Decision Making:
Party and Non-Party

As noted earlier, this "seminar" occurred just two days before we left China. Although it might have been better had we been exposed to the Chinese perception of these terms and concepts at the beginning of our tour, the exposure was valuable in that it enabled us to place information gained earlier into a larger perspective. If the Party operates in accordance with the principles of the mass line, democratic centralism, and collective leadership, it does so in a way that permits it to dominate the entire structure of the educational system. For example, in discussions with our Party-member guides, we learned that high-ranking members of the Ministry of Education are also high-ranking members of the Party who hold positions on or associated with the Central Committee. In fact, we were told that the heads of departments within the ministry are in effect the Party's spokesmen on education. Similarly, we learned that ranking members of provincial educational bureaus are also ranking members of the provincial Party committees who speak, with final authority, on matters of education for the provincial Party apparatus. We observed the same pattern at a people's commune outside Canton, where the people in charge of education were also members of the commune Party committee. Thus, we discovered a pattern of overlapping membership or interlocking directorates which enable the Party to fix policy and then to administer it through a bureaucracy that is not composed entirely of Party members. We were told by our colleagues in Canton that this system permits them to balance the need for centralized control with the flexibility necessary to allow for individual local variations in accord with differing local needs.

School Governance: Revolutionary Committees

During the time of our visit the governing bodies of individual schools were described as revolutionary committees, a form of organization developed during the Cultural Revolution. Just after our departure, while we were still in Hong Kong, we heard that revolutionary committees had been abolished at the university level in favor of a more traditional form embracing leading members of different academic departments and administrative staff under the leadership of a university Party committee. However, since it appears that the principle of operation remains the same as that which obtained during the era of university-level revolutionary committees, we feel justified in including them in this discussion.

The revolutionary committee form is an attempt to provide a governing body for schools, and other units as well, that brings together representatives of different social classes in order to increase the component of democracy in determining and administering school policies. In the Cultural Revolution, revolutionary committees were constituted by members of the People's Liberation Army, representatives of the workers and peasants, and by cadres who worked in the different educational units. Later, however, the army withdrew and the main units of the committees came to include students, teachers, administrators, and representatives of the "masses."

In the schools we visited in China, it seemed to us that the main representatives of the "masses" were individuals who worked around the school in custodial and support jobs. A question on this point produced an admission that this was indeed the case since workers and peasants as a rule found it difficult to allocate time to participate in school governance. Later, during a tour of a middle school in Shanghai, a member of the school's revolutionary committee admitted that workers and peasants frequently lacked the ability to keep abreast of issues and problems faced by the school's teachers and administrative staff because they were present only on a part-time basis. The committee members felt that school governance demanded the attention of a resident and full-time body of personnel who could maintain a day-to-day familiarity with developments in the educational sphere. Our impression was that he thought the idea of mass representation to be good in principle, but that it did not work well in practice.

The primacy of the Party's role was brought home to us in all of the schools that we visited. Two typical examples will illustrate this. At Peking's No. 1 Experimental Primary School, the revolutionary committee that administered the school's affairs was constituted of eleven members who were "elected by teachers, pupils, and the working class." We were told that the members of the working class were janitors, porters, and drivers who were attached to the school. The chairman of the committee was also the principal of the school. The chairman, the vice-chairman, and three other committee members were also members of the Party.

Similarly, at Peking University the governing revolutionary committee was composed of fifty members: ten faculty members and four students, with the remainder from factories and communes directly associated with the university. In this case the "masses" were better able to devote full attention to administrative tasks; in effect, they were members of the university community. The chairman, the vice-chairman, and ten other members of the committee belonged to the Party. Despite the changes in administrative structure wrought by the Cultural Revolution, the Party remains the leading force in school governance.

Centralization and Decentralization in the Administrative Process

Our observations of different schools and universities led us to conclude that there exists an informal division of responsibility between the central and provincial education bureaucracy on the one hand and local school administrators on the other. The decentralized aspect of the administrative process provides local revolutionary committees with the authority to carry out functions within limits set by higher authorities and within the context of the unity provided by the structure of the Party. For example, we noted that in cities the local revolutionary committees were concerned with fiscal support, teacher education, and curriculum development. In Shanghai, for instance, we were somewhat surprised when members of the municipal education office informed us that fees differed from school to school. It was explained that the amount available for support for each school from government sources was fixed and that if an individual school wanted to undertake a program that might involve increased costs, it was the responsibility of the local unit to make up the difference. Because the Shanghai No. 2 Middle School had developed a program of extracurricular activities that was ambitious in comparison to that of other schools, the school's revolutionary committee had decided that an increase in fees was both necessary and justified. We were told that this decision was taken at the school level and then presented to the municipal education office, which rapidly approved the plan. Another example of this latitude for local revolutionary committees was seen on the Huang-tu People's Commune in suburban Shanghai. In this case the school's revolutionary committee had decided that it was practical and desirable to increase the availability of schooling from seven years to ten years. However, state funds (funds from central and provincial sources) were adequate only for the seven-year format. Accordingly, the school revolutionary committee recommended to the commune revolutionary committee that communal resources be allocated to cover the additional costs of capital outlay and teacher salaries. While the plan had to be approved by the municipal education office, it was generated and presented by the local revolutionary committee. Thus, within limits set by higher authorities and with their approval, local units apparently have the authority to adjust fees to suit local needs and circumstances.

We saw the greatest latitude in the area of development of curricular materials where it appeared that local schools, under the supervision of their revolutionary committees, took the lead in compiling, presenting, and evaluating textual materials for use in the local classroom. During a visit to the Nanking Normal College in Kiangsu Province, we learned that a significant number of the teaching and research staff of the college spent time in working with local units to develop these materials. The "curriculum development group" of the local school revolutionary committee would compile ideas and examples to be used in the presentation of mathematics, Chinese language, and "common knowledge" courses and then request that the "experts" of Nanking Normal College evaluate their ideas for pedagogical utility and effectiveness. Working as individual units or teams, local schools thus developed materials that incorporated concrete examples from communes, urban neighborhoods, and the like to provide maximum relevance for the individual student.

We were not able to gather definitive information regarding the scale of such activity in Kiangsu Province or elsewhere in China, but we had the distinct impression that we had come upon a kind of pilot program that may well soon be implemented in other areas of the country. In fact, we were somewhat surprised to see that local school revolutionary committees had such leeway in this area, for the information seemed to fly in the face of other news we heard indicating that China is moving toward a system of unified textual materials. Later we mentioned this apparent contradiction to a leading member of the Shanghai education office. He told us that in fact there was no contradiction, for textual materials were to be unified only in a general sense. He reported that the drive for unification concerned mainly the amount of time spent in instruction in particular subjects rather than identical texts for all schools. He assured us that the context in which specific learning goals were to be presented was to contain ample latitude for presentation in terms of examples derived from the environment of local education units. Thus, a commune that produces tea might have mathematics problems presented in the context of tea production, while another commune that specialized in animal husbandry might well present story problems in terms of increases or decreases in different areas related to animal production. We observed a balance between general standards set by the higher levels of the educational bureaucracy and specific illustrations of those general principles which are formulated by the local revolutionary committee. Unfortunately, we had no opportunity to compare textual and curricular materials from school to school in a systematic way and we were made aware of the fact that the matter of local variation was seriously qualified by the drive to establish national standards for all subject areas. But we accept the notion that local units are left to determine how best to translate national goals into curricular materials for use by local students.

A third area in which we observed latitude was teacher training. It was our impression, gained from all of the schools we visited, that teachers at different levels in the educational system all receive a basic minimum training. However, once they assume their teaching duties, it is expected that they will continue a constant process of in-service education and professional development. Indeed, this was explained to us with some pride by the vice-chairman of Nanking Normal College's revolutionary committee, who also told us that a major responsibility of his teaching and research staff was to be available for consultation in this general area. Since the idea of in-service education was mentioned at every school we visited, we concluded that it is taken seriously and further that it is the local revolutionary committee that assumes primary responsibility in this regard. As noted elsewhere in this volume, each teacher spends Wednesday or Saturday afternoon studying politics and "educational transformation." This latter activity in fact involves evaluating new textbooks, reporting on problems faced in the individual classroom, and general criticism and self-criticism designed to upgrade pedagogical effectiveness. These problems are usually unique to the school in which the continuing education takes place, and the sessions take as their starting point the reality of the environment of each teacher. Therefore the task of fixing the content and the duration of each type of enrichment session is largely in the domain of the individual school revolutionary committee.

Inevitably as we discussed our impressions together in the evenings and over meals, we began to draw comparisons between the revolutionary committees and the school boards of the United States. We concluded that the most significant differences between the American school board and the Chinese revolutionary committee, other than their method of selection, is the Chinese combination of local administration and policy formulation. In the United States there is a desire to separate these two functions. Looking at the revolutionary committee in isolation, this is not clearly discernible. However, it must be kept in mind that those making broad policy decisions, the Party members, also are the leading members of the revolutionary committees.

Party membership comprises less than 5 percent of the population. The strategic location of this 5 percent appears to ensure, in the Chinese view, that the Party line will be transmitted from one level to the next and that there will be continuity in policy development from the top to the bottom in Chinese society. This overlapping and coterminous membership between the main administrative agencies and the Party allows a small number of personnel to control and direct a large establishment. There is in fact very little differentiation between policy formulation and administration.

As we have seen, the Peking No. 1 Experimental Primary School's revolutionary committee was comprised of just less than half Party members. This situation ensures that administrative decisions will correctly reflect the Party line. In short, the cement that holds the system together is the Party.

However, given the small size of the Party's membership, some form of local administrative flexibility is essential. For the central provincial educational authority to attempt to directly control local decisions would require a much larger bureaucracy. For example, the people's commune we visited in Kwangtung Province, with a population of 73,500 and a student enrollment of 15,619 students, had seven people in a "central office" which administered 28 primary and middle schools. The provincial education bureau, which is responsible for more than 11 million students, had less than 100 people on the administrative staff.

The provincial bureau in Kiangsu had approximately 80 employees and was responsible for 52,000 teachers and 13 million students. The bureau provided some services in the areas of finance, teacher training and assignment, higher education, capital construction, and provision of equipment. These examples might be contrasted with our largest state, California, which has 1,400 employees providing services to almost 5 million elementary-secondary students. An effort to duplicate this scope of services and degree of centralization in a nation as large as China not only would imply staggering problems of control, but the effectiveness of such an attempt would be open to serious question. In this case, in our opinion, the theoretical seems to blend very well with the practical. Democratic centralism apparently does allow a certain amount of local flexibility while preserving the basic policy as formulated at higher levels.

The principle of collective leadership also seemed to us to have a certain utility. In the Kwangtung provincial education bureau, although there were less than 100 people employed, the director had seven deputy directors. In the Canton municipal education office there were also seven deputy directors. The No. 1 Experimental Primary School in Peking had a revolutionary committee of eleven members with five vice-chairmen. All of these deputies and vice-chairmen formed the nucleus of the collective leadership of each agency.

On the basis of our observations we noted the emergence of a pattern in how educational decisions seem to be made. The Party is the most important part of the process. Through their apparatus general policy is formulated. Techniques such as the mass line are used in this development. Once the policy is established, the Party plays a vital role in seeing that it is adhered to and that local decisions, while they may reflect local circumstances and conditions, reinforce and support the line as well as official ideology. This all occurs in a highly centralized atmosphere. Collective leadership is then employed to ensure that the mind and ability of several individuals are utilized at the point of decision making. This is done to provide a check against errors in the process. In fact, it is the Chinese Communist Party that makes or controls the educational decision-making process in the People's Republic of China.

CURRICULUM

Gregory R. Anrig

Commissioner of Education, Massachusetts

"Politics is in command of the curriculum," said an official at Peking Normal University. The visits ahead confirmed this consistently. From factory nurseries to university classrooms, the political mission of education in the People's Republic of China was clear — "to develop productive laborers with socialist consciousness."

Consistency was a hallmark of our observations during our eighteen-day journey from Peking to Canton. Our experiences in urban workers' residential quarters and on communes and brigades in the suburban countryside all left us somewhat envious of a system of education that so clearly reflected its mission and which created a classroom environment so supportive of its goals. We felt this to be all the more remarkable since China's educational system has only just become a system of mass education.

Our objective in visiting the People's Republic of China was not to compare its schools with those in the United States. Rather, we were there to learn about Chinese society and Chinese education as it has developed since 1949. We saw a huge country which describes itself as being in the process of "building socialism," a process that perforce engenders great change in the pattern of Chinese life. These changes are particularly significant in the area of education. Thus, it rapidly became clear that if we were even to begin to understand the logic of the Chinese system, it would be necessary to view it within the social and political context signaled by the rubric "socialist transformation."

Because China is committed to socialist development, education is an instrument of national policy. In contrast to the highly decentralized system of education in the United States, questions of how much education for whom and in what form are policies decided "at the highest levels" of the State Council. Education is a matter of national politics.

This is witnessed by the number of times education has emerged as an issue of political debate. For example, local hosts at the scene of each visit and the guides who traveled with us all were eager to tell us about the turbulent Great Proletarian Cultural Revolution which began in 1966 and was not officially declared ended until the Eleventh National Congress of the Chinese Communist Party in August 1977. At Peking University the Cultural Revolution was described as a radical and violent manifestation of disagreement over what kind of educational priorities best served to fulfill the goals of the late Chairman Mao Tse-tung and Chinese communism. Those who participated proudly described their participation in actions aimed at purging from Chinese society what was considered to be growing elitism and classism. Now, they told us, national policy under Chairman Hua Kuo-feng is shifting toward a drive for modernization — of industry, of agriculture, of science and technology, and of national defense. This requires educational stability and an emphasis on developing technological capacity. The result, as we saw at Peking University and elsewhere, is a growing concern for standards, reintroduction of the competitive examination system, and a national drive to advance science at all levels of learning. However, even though the change potentially is dramatic and far-reaching, there is consistency. Politics remains a central component of the curriculum.

The Chinese View of Politics

It was not until we were well into our trip and only after

many hours of discussion with our escorts and local hosts that we came to the realization that in China the term "politics" conveys a set of meanings that differs markedly from our own notion of politics as the interplay of opposing forces within the context of a set of accepted rules and procedures. Politics is more than competition. Politics is building socialism.

We never received the benefit of a concise statement concerning the meaning of the term "building socialism." However, in our internal discussions we were able to piece together from comments made by officials at all levels a preliminary idea of the unity of politics and building socialism. This extremely sketchy idea is outlined below.

During an outing to the Ming Tombs we heard that building socialism requires more than just increasing China's productive capacity in the areas of industry, agriculture, science and technology, and national defense. It requires that the process of national regeneration itself be conducted in a way such that basic attitudes toward the quality of life undergo change. By participation in the process of modernization and social change the Chinese people are to develop a set of attitudes and behavior patterns that reflect rejection of the idea of achieving fulfillment in terms of the individual and acceptance of the notion that fulfillment occurs within the context of the development of the larger society. This means that the individual must assign new values to continuing social roles. He must learn, for example, that there is no difference in the social value of mental as distinct from manual labor. He or she must reject particularistic class views in favor of a broader view of society as a whole and — since classes have social power — this, we were told, is a matter of politics. Politics involves class struggle. It is of course easy for individuals such as the members of our delegation to dismiss such talk as mere propaganda or as the logical end result of years of political indoctrination. However, whatever its source, this idea forms a part of the reality of life for all of the Chinese with whom we spoke. It is at least spoken of with great seriousness and it does seem to be seen as an ideal worth struggling to achieve.

We also learned that politics refers to the extent to which individuals have successfully internalized this view of life. Chinese must demonstrate in concrete ways that the good of the whole society is what motivates individual initiatives in the classroom or in the workplace. Politics also refers to a way of looking at the world. In this sense, politics is coterminous with ideology.

Finally, and central to all that has been related thus far, is our realization that in practice the Chinese regard willingness to follow the Party's lead and direction in all things as a primary indicator of the state of individual ideological development. Discussions with Party members in Peking and Shanghai indicated that while criticism and comment form an integral aspect of Party life, the Chinese Communists regard themselves as the custodians of the values of Chinese society. Government policy and Party policy are therefore identical. Politics, we learned, involves loyalty to the Party.

Thus, to say that politics is in command of the curriculum is to say two things about Chinese education. First, Chinese education is designed to impart to members of the society a set of skills that will enable the individual to make an effective and useful contribution to economic development and modernization. Second, and of greater importance, we learned that Chinese education also seeks to inculcate a certain world view that governs the motivation of the individual and which also provides a context for the application of acquired skills. The authoritative arbiter of how this will be done is the Chinese Communist Party. Chinese education is political education.

Political Symbols

In all, during our brief stay, we visited four kindergartens, three primary schools, one lower middle school, two upper middle schools, and five colleges and universities. The small number of institutions plus the fact that these were selected for us by our hosts makes generalization difficult. But, nonetheless, there are some areas in which similarities between units were striking. Because of this we feel justified in discussing them here.

If, as noted above, the centrality of politics is a consistent theme in our observations and discussions, the symbols of politics are an ever present aspect of each school's physical environment and of activities within the classroom. In all cases these symbols are related to concrete matters of national policy. For example, the otherwise spartan aspect of each classroom is relieved by the presence of photographs. Above and to the left of the teacher's desk is placed a portrait of Mao Tsetung. Immediately opposite, to the right as one faces the teacher's desk, is a portrait of Chairman Hua Kuo-feng. This serves the obvious purpose of identifying Hua with Mao, but the arrangement is also clearly designed to acquaint the students with Hua. In every case, Hua's name appears beneath his picture. Of course, no such caption is necessary in the case of Mao. Beneath the photographs is placed a quotation from Mao, enjoining students to "study diligently; make constant progress." Other photographs, usually along one of the side walls, are of Marx, Engels, Lenin, and Stalin. Interestingly, Stalin is always pictured in the uniform of a Marshall of the Soviet Union, indicating that he is to be most remembered for his military role in repelling "fascist aggression against the Soviet motherland" rather than for his contribution to Soviet domestic politics. Indeed, conversations with teachers and local hosts indicated an extreme sensitiveness to the problem of balancing an awareness of Stalin's admitted mistakes against the need to recognize his value as a positive symbol in China's continuing dispute with the Soviet leadership. In the same way, school courtyards and college campuses all are centered upon a large statue of Mao. As a result of these omnipresent statues, photographs, and quotations, Chinese students at all levels are constantly reminded of the originators of the ideology they study and of why they study it.

Similarly, in the No. 2 Peking Kindergarten, students pointed to a small-scale model of the Taching oil complex, explained the functions of each of the different subunits, and then described how the function of each part related to the operation of the whole. In this way, we were told, young people learn about the proper line for industrial development and are sensitized to problems in the process of industrial growth. Through our interpreters we also learned that the students are able to state how the arrangement of the complex and the leadership of the Party combine to enable Taching to reach its production goals so well. An identical purpose is served by photographs and models of Tachai Commune, which serves as the model for agricultural development in the People's Republic. Here students look at "before and after" photographs of Tachai and explain how these remarkable changes have come about. In every case, the youngsters we met noted the linkage between the correct line of the Party, the instructions of the "Great Leader Chairman Mao" and the "Wise Leader Chairman Hua," and the results achieved at Tachai. In these ways, children of kindergarten and primary-school age receive exposure to the direction and content of national policies.

As we visited larger numbers of schools we encountered other more subtle and more sophisticated examples of the use of political symbols. One example struck all of us in this regard. At the No. 2 Peking Kindergarten, five- and six-year-old children entertained us with a performance of music and dance. One program depicted a naval unit "on duty" on the "high seas," "protecting the fatherland." A young boy dressed as a naval officer peered into the distance and spied an approaching "enemy." He called the crew to battle stations and his fellow performers responded with alacrity. The group formed itself into a representation of a naval cannon and moved back and forth in the manner of a gun being fired rapidly. The accompanying drum lent an air of verisimilitude by providing the sound of explosions. After several minutes of this "combat" the enemy was destroyed, an event which occasioned much rejoicing by the members of the crew. Apart from the precision of the dance movements, we were most impressed by the clear message of patriotism and need to mobilize for national defense implicit in the performance. However, we were also puzzled by the lack

of specificity concerning the nature of the threatening enemy.
When discussing this with our interpreters later, we were told
that the exercise was designed to inculcate the concept of the
need for vigilance and national defense generally and that it was
not designed to build consciousness of a particular danger from
a specific quarter. Our interpreters also admitted, however,
that the same performance would have identified the United
States as the "enemy" prior to 1972-73 and that the Soviet Union
might still be cast in this role.

Another number in the same program had kindergarten students in the role of truck drivers hauling grain from a commune to the grain warehouse. The words of the song emphasized the need to learn to understand machinery and the importance of delivering each little bit of grain in perfect condition to where it is needed. The important symbols here are of course the truck with its implications for modernization and grain which reflects the importance of the agricultural base as the source of national wealth. Woven through the performance is an emphasis on conscientious performance of duty in discharging important tasks.

A final example, and one which we saw in kindergartens, primary schools, and lower middle schools alike, involved the symbol of China's minority nationalities. Although the Tibetans were most often chosen in these presentations, Mongols and Uigurs were also featured. In one of these performances a young girl played the role of a "Mao Tse-tung Thought" propagandist spreading the news of publication of volume five of Mao's selected works among China's national minorities. This symbol provides students with awareness of the fact that China is a multinational country and, further, that the minorities need to be integrated fully into the pattern of Chinese life. By depicting the joy with which the latest volume was received, the themes of national unity and respect are symbolized as an important part of the individual student's concern.

The examples noted above by no means provide an exhaustive list of those that we saw. Rather, they are the ones that made the most dramatic impression upon the members of our group.

Also, it is necessary to remind the reader that we are not able to state with certainty that these symbols are universally utilized in schools throughout the country. However, they seemed to us to be so basic to China's emerging priorities that we feel justified in noting them here. In the same way, we of course have no way of knowing the extent to which the messages of these symbols are actually internalized by China's young people and how long the internalization may last once it is achieved. However, it is clear that political symbols are an integral aspect of the school environment and, further, that political symbols form a significant part of the content of the Chinese curriculum.

Politics and Teaching Methodology

Class sizes we observed in the Chinese schools averaged forty-five pupils at all grade levels. Students sat in double rows behind fixed desks. The main teaching methods observed were group recitation and individual responses to teacher questions (with the student standing and answering in a clear and loud voice). In lower grades, children folded their hands behind their backs and leaned on them when not reciting. Academic instruction in the People's Republic is a group experience in a teacher-directed and tightly disciplined setting. Only in arts, music, and physical education did we see individual and small group activities with lots of movement, laughter, and self-direction. In China the teacher is the custodian of the body of knowledge that is to be learned; he or she is expected to impart this to the class. Students in turn are expected to demonstrate control of knowledge by "giving" it back to the teacher.

Within this methodological setting, instructional exercises reinforce political themes or, put differently, instruction in what we in the United States would call substantive areas is often couched in political terms. For example, in the Peking No. 1 Experimental Primary School, a fourth-grade English-language class required students to point to pictures of a city and farm "before and after Liberation," showing how conditions had improved. We noted that both questions and responses seemed to follow a set pattern and, interestingly, on one occasion students seemed to answer a question that was different from the one that had been asked. Most of the "differences" noted related to cleanliness, regularity of terraces and paddy fields, extended provision of services, and general improvement in livelihood. While students obviously learn a number of English words and sentence patterns, they also receive a short course in the impressive physical changes in Chinese society since 1949.

In the same school we observed a third-grade lesson in Chinese. Here the teacher wrote certain characters on the blackboard and asked the students to use them in simple sentences. The words "want," "future," "serve," and the like were designed to stimulate the students to think of themselves in the future. Students responded with such statements as "I want to be a soldier"; "I want to be a barefoot doctor"; "In the future I will be an astronaut"; and "I will serve the people." In one or two cases where the student had forgotten, the teacher added the phrase, "to serve the people." Thus, while the students learn Chinese words appropriate to their grade and general cultural level, they also receive a clear message about future goals and expectations.

In Shanghai's No. 2 Middle School an English lesson began with a reminder of "why we study." Students and teacher recited in loud voices: "We study English for the revolution, the world revolution. Karl Marx says language is a weapon in the revolution of life." In the Nanking Normal College students were asked to give concrete examples of how the Gang of Four had sabotaged the correct line of Chairman Mao Tse-tung in a number of areas related to industry, agriculture, and education. Again we had the impression that the students and teachers alike were reciting a series of set questions and answers, which led us to wonder just how useful such instruction actually was. However, in informal conversations with the college students we all found that they were able to carry on lively and spirited conversations at their respective levels and that if they exhibited any deficiencies, they were those associated with an inability to practice English with native speakers of English. Apparently the system works.

Textbooks we noted were more like inexpensive paperbacks than the colorful texts found in American classrooms. This may be a function of the fact that paper is a precious commodity in China and, more importantly, a result of the fact that since the Cultural Revolution China has seen an explosion of "experimental" texts. Only now are the Chinese moving to standardized materials. In a third-year English class at Nanking Normal College we saw a mimeographed version of Dickens' <u>Great Expectations</u> in which sections of the story were given such headings as "I Rob My Family" and "I Enter the Bourgeois Life."

Since it forms an integral aspect of teaching methodology, we also inquired about grouping policy. School officials responded that they do not believe in the separation or grouping of slower students. They feel this would have a psychological effect upon the students that would make them feel inferior. Similarly, they noted that it would also have a negative ideological (political) effect in that the slower students might feel that they have less to contribute than the brighter students and also that the brighter students might fall prey to feelings of pride and arrogance. Here again practice in the classroom is consistent with the political objectives of the society at large. All work is socially useful and all can and should make what contribution they can. Those who are able to do more should help those who are able to do less.

Virtually everyone with whom we spoke, from the Minister of Education to primary-school teachers on suburban communes, cited the importance of linking classroom education with productive labor. However, our experience raised many questions regarding the real definition of physical labor in the educational process and its effect on the development of students. We noted that there are many kinds of labor assignments and that these seem to be directed toward fulfillment of different purposes. We were not able to come to any set of systematic conclusions except at the most general level.

We learned that all students in primary schools spend four days per year in factory or farm work and four days per year in military drill during grades 1-3. Usually these experiences occur in regular rotation. In grades 4-5 this is increased to six days per year in each activity. This labor may occur in factories or on farms that are formally associated with the school, that simply happen to be close to the school, or in places that seem to need additional labor input. Military drill at the primary-school level involves members of the People's Liberation Army coming to the school to give instruction in drill, military discipline, and "the importance of obeying orders." We derived no sense of the intensity of these experiences, although our observations confirm the impression that Chinese students are well ordered and well disciplined. We were told that students in upper primary grades learn how to "pack up" and bivouac in the field. At the middle-school level, students continue military experience for two or three days annually, but work experience in the factory or farm is increased to two periods per week throughout the year.

As noted earlier, we encountered a problem in attempting to sort out and evaluate the effect of this kind of experience. The schools we saw were all either in urban centers or in suburban communes and were clearly well developed in terms of facilities and historical experience. In general we found that neither primary students nor the primary schools receive remuneration for factory or farm work. Labor, it was said, is a part of education and treated much like a regular aspect of the curriculum. However, we noted at least one exception to this rule: the middle schools we visited either had factories located on the school premises or had a special relationship with factories in the immediate neighborhood. They also had a special connection with readily accessible communes in the area. In these cases labor was led by older workers and peasants, but it was difficult to determine whether labor is undertaken to provide an added dimension to certain courses or for more general purposes of consciousness raising, or both. In some cases the proceeds of student labor reverted to the school, such as at Nanking Power

Upper Middle School, where more than 300,000 yuan in annual proceeds revert to the Ministry of Petrochemicals to which the school is attached and from which the school receives its annual budget of 340,000 yuan. Thus, in some cases labor appears to be a part of the curriculum and assumes some of the characteristics of just another course, while in others it appears to fulfill the requirements of wage labor as defined in communist ideology. This in turn raises questions at the theoretical level, at least about the effect that the labor experience can have upon the development of individual students, for they are never placed in a position where they become dependent upon the proceeds of their labor.

However, one conclusion can be ventured. Work experience serves a different purpose in China's schools than in America's. Here the aim of work experience is to help the student acquire skills, knowledge, and attitudes designed to open up career opportunities and to enlighten the choice of careers. In Chinese schools, whatever the real effect in practical terms, labor has a value in itself and is defined as productive labor. It is only by direct participation in productive labor that students can develop a feeling of comradeship with the workers, peasants, and soldiers of Chinese society. Work experience in China thus has a group and political goal, rather than a goal of individual advancement as in our own system. Because of the importance of this political goal in Chinese education, we came to appreciate the logic of work experience as a planned part of schooling from the earliest classes in primary grades through university-level education. We also recognized that the labor experience has an observable impact on the student while in the school environment. But because of the different and overlapping formats for labor participation, we were less clear about the long-range effect upon the development of the individual student in relation to continuing goals of moral-political development.

Politics and the Curriculum

On the basis of what has been said thus far, it is clear that politics enters the curriculum in different ways. First, symbols are utilized to present certain themes, messages, and desired behavior patterns. Second, these symbols and themes provide a context for the presentation of more "substantive" aspects of the learning process. Third, politics in its broadest sense enters the curriculum because of the connection of the classroom experience with the process of productive labor in its many different forms. Finally, politics is important in that it forms an integral component of the curriculum as a separate and distinct subject of study.

Much has been said of late about a reduction in the political component of Chinese education in all of its aspects in favor of a return to the substantive basics. However, our observations indicate that this judgment may be premature and even that it may be erroneous. It was our impression from discussions with education leaders in Peking, Kiangsu, Shanghai, Chekiang, and Canton that such changes may more likely be ones of degree and emphasis, with a result somewhere midway between the perceived excesses of the pre-1966 period and the educational upheaval of the Cultural Revolution period. All of our informants reaffirmed the fact that politics will continue to be an important part of the curriculum.

This assertion received added credence when the comments of leading provincial level educators are combined and synthesized to produce a typical curriculum. At the primary-school level (grades 1-5) this includes:

Chinese language	Music
Arithmetic	Physical education
Political education	Labor education
Drawing and painting	

Calligraphy, English, and "general knowledge" (history, geography, and natural sciences) are added in grades 4 and 5.

At the secondary level (grades 6-8) the curriculum week is as follows [the number in parentheses denotes class periods per week]:

Chinese (6)
Mathematics (6)
Music (1)
Physical education (2)
English (3)
Political education (2)

Agriculture (2)
Drawing (2)
Geography (2)
History (2)
Work experience (9)

In grades 7 and 8, chemistry and physics (3 periods per week each) replace geography, history, and drawing.

We noted that the subject "political education" is required at all primary and secondary grades. Provincial officials described the content of this as follows:

Kindergarten: Simple ideas about the Party, country, collectives, and the revolutionary tradition. Students learn by emulating such models as Lei Feng (a soldier who selflessly served the people without telling them his name). Students perform tasks around the school and learn how to help others.

Primary grades: General knowledge of politics. Education for morality (defined as love of the motherland, love of the Party, love of Chairman Mao, and love of the people).

Middle-school grades: Basic themes of Marxism and Leninism. Simplified history of social evolution; knowlege of political economy; knowledge of dialectical materialism. Introduction to pure communist theory.

It should be noted that labor and military components of the curriculum increase as the grade level increases.

In discussions with these provincial educators as well as with teachers in local schools, we became aware of four major approaches to political education as a formal course of study. Naturally, these approaches also apply to the other means of introducing politics into the curriculum. First, formal political study involves the use of the symbols mentioned earlier. Second, there is a constant use of models of revolutionary virtue, such as the student-soldier-worker named Lei Feng, for emulation by individual students. Third, we noted the practice of community involvement in political education. Older workers and peasants, we were told, came to schools to contrast the past with the present and to serve as living examples of the improvements wrought since the Liberation. Finally, formal political study involves the use of texts. We were impressed by the fact that these different methods or approaches to formal political education were varied according to grade level, but also by the fact that elements of each approach exist at all levels. Emulation, while a major technique at the primary level, is also used at the middle-school level, and community involvement seems to occur at all levels. Thus, political education in the formal sense draws upon a wide range of social supports and forms an enduring aspect of the total curriculum. We feel that in the future it will be necessary to look at the relative mix of approaches to formal and informal political education in order to assess the relative continuity of politics in the curriculum. However, even if political education does become "watered down" in the long run, the long tradition of such training, the precedents for its upgrading in the Cultural Revolution, and the fact that Chinese families have come to accept the inevitability if not the desirability of politics in the curriculum ensures that Chinese education will continue to have a highly significant political component.

ADMISSIONS

Louis R. Smerling

President, National Association of State Boards of Education

Of the issues connected with education in China, none is so sensitive within the bureaucracy and so controversial among students as the manner in which candidates for entrance to certain secondary and all postsecondary institutions are chosen, for few things can effect greater change or offer greater opportunity to a Chinese youth than to become one of the few allowed to continue education beyond the eighth grade. Ironically, few things in China have varied so widely and changed so often over the past few decades as admissions policies.

Just one week before we landed in Peking on October 28, China's Minister of Education, Liu Hsi-yao, announced the most recent policy change. Following a national work conference on the enrollment of students for institutions of higher learning, held in Peking on September 25, 1977, the Ministry of Education began announcing enrollment reforms on October 20. The new method of selection of college freshmen, we were told, was designed to guarantee that academically superior students get first crack at enrollment in the best schools. Simultaneously the new policy was supposed to prevent the reemergence of an intellectual elite of the sort that reportedly characterized Chinese campuses prior to 1966, when the Cultural Revolution opened the doors to the sons and daughters of peasants, workers, and soldiers (regardless of educational ability) and began to shut out high achievers.

The new policy came as quite a shock to the more than 20 million prospective college entrants. No middle-school graduate had been required to take an entrance examination since 1974; most youth had not been subjected to a formal academic entrance examination since 1966. Yet, within two months of the announcement, all were to undergo a comprehensive exam. Because of the announced reforms, bookstores were jammed with long lines of candidates during our stay and libraries were filled to the brim with students trying to cram several years of schooling into a little more than six weeks. For many it would be their first "big" exam. The realization that this battery of tests could alter their lives must have been incredibly agonizing and worrisome, even to the brightest of students. It certainly was foremost in the minds of many students we met. As it turned out, only 5.7 million students of the 20 million eligible wound up taking the exam in December. Of that figure, a mere 300,000 received final approval and went on to enroll, making the ratio of the number of eligibles to the number admitted nearly 70 to 1. In the United States, where many single states annually enroll more than 300,000 freshmen, where half of all high-school graduates enter college, and where at any given time up to 5 percent of the population (compared with .04 percent in China) is enrolled in postsecondary education, those figures are limited indeed.

Perhaps even more grim than the quantity of China's college education (i.e., the number of students) is the quality of education the average student receives. In Shanghai our hosts related to us the depressing results of a recent series of exams administered to a crop of college graduates who had already been assigned careers in the city. Although the exams were high-school level, 67 percent failed mathematics, 70 percent failed physics, and 76 percent of the college graduates could not pass an upper middle-school chemistry test. These results were among the factors that prompted Professor Chou P'ei-yuan of Peking University to accuse the so-called Gang of Four of "wasting an entire generation of intellects" during our meeting with him on the university campus. It will take until the mid-1980s before

China is able to graduate a class of college students who have been through middle school and higher education without being influenced — and held back — by the anti-intellectualism of the era of the Cultural Revolution and its aftermath. Thus, the full effects of any new education policy, including admissions, will be felt only gradually by the society as a whole. The fact that educational standards have been raised does not mean that China will begin to graduate well-educated students immediately; that process will still take another five to ten years.

It should be kept firmly in mind that, even in this sensitive area, the fact that major reforms have been instated does not necessarily mean that all policies associated with the Cultural Revolution are null and void. On the contrary, China retains its commitment to open education, even though it made this commitment at the height of the Cultural Revolution and even though the new practice of using the results of an academic examination for admissions would seem to mitigate against open education. Our hosts repeatedly emphasized, in fact, that the pre-1966 practice of using exams as the exclusive criterion for selection had unwisely favored students who for reasons of family background or level of environmental sophistication were better able to take examinations. Specifically, we were told that this meant the children of workers, peasants, and minority races were too easily made victims of "examination discrimination." Because they had fewer advantages, these students were almost automatically unable to compete on a par with those students whose backgrounds were more privileged. In this way, the Chinese told us, a gap had developed between China's urban and rural areas and also within the urban areas where children of cadres, army personnel, and members of the former bourgeoisie predominated. The effect of such a policy, the Chinese emphasized, was that those admitted to the more developed units of the educational system separated themselves from Chinese society as a whole. In a word, the educational system was a breeding ground for social "elitism."

The Cultural Revolution had attempted to offer an antidote to elitism. But, by denying the validity of such academic pursuits as examinations, it had apparently gone too far. As the Chinese were fond of telling us, "The remedy may have been curing the disease, but it was killing the patient."

If our hosts were candid about the contradiction of keeping certain Cultural Revolution reforms even while lambasting the Gang of Four, who had essentially engineered the Cultural Revolution, they were enthusiastic in describing the new system. They were uniformly certain that the new way of doing things would solve the problems of the past by creating a neat and delicate balance between the pre-1966 way, which clearly favored "experts," and the Cultural Revolution way, which judged "redness" more important. This juxtaposition is aptly described by the Chinese as the debate of "red vs. expert." Over the past two decades in China, each side of this debate has held various degrees of sway over the other at any particular time. The two have never been in balance. The current goal of admissions policies in China is therefore to admit students who, for the first time, are both fully "red" and fully "expert."

What is offered in this chapter is a report on the new admissions policies as they bear upon the different levels of the educational system. We will attempt to report as faithfully as we can what we were told and what we observed. Our questions and doubts, as well as the responses of our hosts, will also be noted. While it is too soon to tell whether or not the current system is striking the hoped-for balance, we can set forth the perceptions and expectations of our Chinese counterparts. Before beginning, we should once again stress that our experiences were limited to urban and suburban schools and that our comments on rural institutions and practices are based upon statements made by our Chinese guides, interpreters, and local hosts.

Nurseries, Kindergartens, and Primary Schools

The fall of the Gang of Four has done nothing to effect changes in admissions at the lowest levels of schools in China. Admission to nurseries, kindergartens, and primary schools remains limited only by the availability of facilities. In general, admission to these facilities is available on request.

We observed that nurseries and kindergartens are usually located at or close to the work place of at least one of the parents. As a rule, children of primary-school age enter schools that are closest to their place of residence, although in some cases work units such as factories, government office complexes, and universities may have primary schools on their premises. One of our interpreters informed us that she had attended an integrated primary-secondary school at which she had boarded when she was a child, but that such schools had all but disappeared in the welter of reforms instituted after 1966. (An interesting offshoot of this conversation revealed that boarding school had deprived her of the chance to learn to cook. This, she said, is usually learned at home and, since she had not lived with her family when growing up, she had not learned to prepare any but the simplest dishes.)

We were somewhat surprised by the fact that most students are expected to pay fees to cover the costs related to their schooling. While the fees associated with transportation, food, and books usually represent a miniscule portion of the average household budget, it struck us as unusual that a socialist country should require any payment at all. Fees are charged primarily in order to keep accounting and purchasing procedures to a minimum. It is, we were told, more efficient for each school to provide basic services on its own than it would be to create a bureaucratic organization to provide these same services. Secondly, there is a feeling in China that parents should bear a direct financial responsibility for the education of their children.

During a long automobile ride from Yangchow to Nanking, our guide Mr. Hu gave us a thumbnail sketch of the "needs-analysis" method of calculating how much students pay for their education. According to Mr. Hu, about 30 percent of all students, elementary through postsecondary, receive scholarships from the schools they attend. The average cost of education per child being $7.50 a month in urban areas and $6.00 a month in rural areas, city schools give assistance to students from urban families who earn an average of $12 a month per family member and rural schools give to families averaging $10 income a month per member. In other words, a family of four living in Peking and earning $48 a month would be ineligible for a scholarship. Families earning progressively less than that amount receive progressively larger scholarships until the full "cost" for a child from a low-income family is covered by the scholarship. Ironically, the number of students eligible for scholarships multiplied by the average amount of money needed exceeds the amount of money available. The fact that the United States has similar problems in fully funding its financial aid programs seemed to be of little consolation to the Chinese. Mr. Hu informed us that this elementary needs test is the same for all levels of school, right through postgraduate studies, although scholarships tend to be larger in colleges and universities, where costs are higher.

Whenever we raised the question of what happens when a family cannot afford to pay and no scholarship is available, our hosts responded that such cases rarely occur, that there is always a way to take care of such difficulties, and that no family is ever asked to be one of the few families in a school to feel a pinch. In cases of minor funding gaps, the difference is spread evenly throughout all families with children enrolled in the school; in the worst cases, school administrators simply reduce their budget to the point at which they are able to treat all students and families equally.

Middle School

For several reasons our delegation experienced difficulty developing a picture of middle-school admissions policies. First, different kinds of middle-school "formats" seem to coexist in China at present. The basic model, as explained to us by cadres in Peking and Shanghai, embraces a pattern of five years of primary school and three years of lower middle school followed by two years of upper middle school. However, one primary school we visited in Peking included a sixth year. We also visited a school in Shanghai that is an integrated ten-year school in which differences between the various levels that are standard in other middle schools are not clearly defined. Second, the revival of what is known as the "key schools" system further divides middle-school admissions criteria into standards for students with high potential and standards for ordinary students. Third, accessibility and duration of education at this level differ according to location within the country. For example, the Minister of Education and several directors of provincial education bureaus informed us that ten years of education is universally available in most of China's major urban centers but that the length of schooling in the countryside is very uneven. According to Minister Liu, some rural areas have achieved the goal of seven years of universal education but most have not; this remains a target that will not be reached for some time to come.

It is in these areas, where upper middle-school candidates exceed the number of places available for enrollment, that the academic entrance examination often first begins to affect the entry of China's students into China's schools. We have seen that admission requirements for primary schools are pro forma, automatic, and do not include academic exams. The same is true in middle schools located in areas where that level of education is available to all applicants. But once a school's potential student population is greater than the school's capacity, academic examinations are utilized to conduct an initial screening of candidates, with political attitude and physical health operating as second- and third-echelon criteria.

Although not used for admissions purposes, the same sort of academic examination is often given to students in areas with full enrollment. Here the test results are used to determine whether the student has either a special problem or a special aptitude. Problems can then, theoretically, be overcome. Special talents can be channeled into pursuits tailored to make maximum use of the unusual ability.

Since they can be used in this manner as a pedagogical device to define levels at which students operate, admissions examinations are also given to students eligible for entry into the "key schools" system mentioned above.

Key Schools

Key schools are usually financed in part at least by the national, provincial, or local government. They are designed to provide an environment in which students who excel can benefit by the introduction of new materials and teaching methods by highly trained teachers. Key schools existed in China prior to 1966, after which time the concept was condemned as elitist and at odds with the values embraced by the Cultural Revolution. Since 1966 these schools have functioned as ordinary neighborhood schools.

During our delegation's visit key schools were on their way back. We were told that students will be assigned to key schools on the basis of three criteria: first, academic excellence based on the results of an examination (which was being developed) and grades in school; second, political-moral awareness; and third, adequate physical condition. Each criterion will be assessed sequentially; failure at any stage is cause for elimination from further consideration. Those students who pass the examination will be rated on how well they get along with their peers, whether or not they voluntarily assist their classmates and participate in labor assignments, whether they are "respectful" in relation to teachers and public property, and whether they manifest such signs of activism as participation in the Little Red Soldiers, the Red Guards, or the Communist Youth League. This information, we were told, will be generated and provided by the teachers, staff, and students of the school attended. Our impression was that each student will be rated according to these criteria and that this information will then be forwarded to the key school, where the final evaluation will be made. Since the academic exam is given before the political assessment takes place, even students with outstanding political aptitude and backgrounds will not be able to continue their education unless they can first pass the test.

Under the key schools plan, a number of representative schools, universities, and colleges of various kinds are given the opportunity to choose and enroll students with superior academic ability. Key schools also have more competent faculties and better teaching facilities, made possible by government aid. Simply put, their function is to raise educational standards for select students and at the same time to use their own advanced and often innovative experiences as a guide for other educational institutions.

Our group advanced the argument that such criteria could lead to a revival of elitism and that it might be difficult to ensure that political tests do not become a mere formality. Our hosts admitted that such developments are entirely possible but assured us that the lessons of the Great Proletarian Cultural Revolution had been learned and China would not fall prey again to an educational admissions policy that simply "takes the best and leaves the rest." Interestingly, it was apparent from the answers we received at institutions of higher education that this question is more pressing at this level than at the middle-school level. Perhaps this is because academic excellence is of less importance as a criterion for admission at lower levels where openings are more numerous and competition less rigorous.

Thus middle-school admissions policies seem designed to rank students according to academic ability and then to assign the upper ranks to the best schools and channel average students into separate areas of special aptitude or interest. Generally, students who do not complete the process of being admitted to a middle schoool are immediately tapped for employment of different kinds and have little, if any, further opportunity to receive an education.

Universities and Colleges

During our brief meeting with him one evening in the International Club in Peking, Minister of Education Liu Hsi-yao's most interesting remarks pertained to the spate of admissions reforms he had just made public. Minister Liu, a tall man who appeared to us to be both overworked and anxious, was most emphatic in asserting that the examinations would be the key aspect of the new approach to admissions.

Other important aspects of the October 21 announcement provided that the following categories of students would be eligible to take exams:

a) all upper middle-school graduates who are single and younger than twenty-five;

b) upper middle-school students who have "rich experience" or who have "scored achievements";

c) upper middle-school graduates of the classes of 1966 and 1967, whether married or single, and "preferably" younger than thirty (twenty-five-year-old graduates would have been the class of 1970 and therefore eligible; the classes of 1968 and 1969 were not eligible for the December 1977 exam, but in April 1978 were made eligible for all subsequent examinations);

d) lower middle-school graduates, who from 1966 had been allowed to enter college if they had appropriate "life experience," would no longer be eligible to enroll in higher education.

The examinations themselves were to emphasize common knowledge and to judge problem-solving abilities. The famous "blank paper," which became a cause célèbre after a student named Chang T'ieh-sheng refused to write an examination during the Cultural Revolution, would no longer suffice. Though similar in intent, examinations in the different provinces and cities would not be standardized; instead they were to be prepared at the municipal or provincial level (no attempt to standardize tests was made until the spring of 1978). Three kinds of tests were available: liberal arts, natural sciences, and foreign languages.

The selection procedure was described to us as follows:

1. The Basic Level

Students submit applications to their own basic units (communes, factories, mines, government offices, schools, etc.). An application contains the student's top two or three preferences of subjects and schools. After the initial screening has been completed, the basic level is asked to file a report on the political attitude of candidates.

2. The County and School District Level

Eligible applicants are referred by basic units to this level. Here the rural county or urban district educational administrative organ administers the tests provided by the province or city. Without reviewing the results, this level then forwards the completed exams to the next higher level.

3. The Provincial, Municipal, or Autonomous Region Level

    a. At this level, test results are reviewed and drastic cuts are made. Optimally, once this stage is completed, the number of qualified applicants remaining will be approximately twice as many as the number of college openings.
    b. Quotas are enforced at this level, contrary to the practice after 1966 by which basic units made decisions according to assigned quotas. We were told that quotas are used to ensure that each sector of Chinese society is proportionally represented in the pool of eligible college entrants.
    c. Theoretically, 20 to 30 percent of all college openings are reserved for upper middle-school graduates who, again contrary to standard practice, are allowed to enter college directly from middle school without having to experience two years of manual labor in the interim. The Cultural Revolution mandated that all college entrants have this minimum. The new policy retains this qualification for only 70 or 80 percent of the students entering college.
    d. The province or municipality then asks each applicant it is about to pass judgment on to undergo a physical examination, usually at a county or district hospital.
    e. Simultaneously, basic units are asked to report on the

political attitude of applicants who have passed the test.

f. All three reports (academic exam, political assessment, physical exam) are assembled and submitted to the schools concerned.

g. Finally, the individual school makes the last review of all applications, selects what number of students it can take, and issues admissions notices to the fortunate few.

Our efforts to get beyond the formal explanation of the examination and selection process were marked by frustration. Invariably, the topic of conversation turned to our group's feeling that elitism would be a natural outgrowth of the system. Virtually the only safeguards in the otherwise subjective selection formula are the quotas used to guarantee a modicum of ethnic and geographic balance and the percentage of students who are still required to work for two years after middle school before college. Beyond this, it seemed to us, the system is open to all manner of manipulation, cronyism, and entry through the "back door." Particularly prone to bending for personal gain, we felt, is the political evaluation given each prospective college student.

During our walk with them through the gardens at the Running Tiger Spring in Hangchow (Chekiang Province), we challenged our local hosts with the assertion that the political test was too abstract to be of use in a country as large as China. How could they hope to develop objective measures of political manifestation? "Politics is not abstract," our guides responded. First, the class origin of an applicant is a concrete factor that no one can change. Class origins are identified in order to distinguish students of worker and peasant families and give them certain privileges while denying these same privileges to students of less revolutionary classes, such as the former bourgeoisie, landlords, rich peasants, and former members of the Kuomintang (Nationalist Chinese) government. Second, examiners also have access to school records which include information on student behavior, participation in political activities, etc. Third, since most students have been working for a minimum of two years, they have on-the-job records of how they apply politics in their everyday lives. Finally, the basic unit to which a prospective student is attached prepares a written report on the applicant's attitudes toward work, relationship with peers, and attitudes toward struggle, criticism, and revolution. In sum, the political test as it was described to us is supposed to involve a great deal of "solid" data on individual behavior that has been collected over a period of years.

Perhaps the best defense we heard of the political exam, however, was that the academic test is far more important in the evaluation process. Only students who pass the test, for instance, are judged politically. Were it vice versa, politics would be in command. As it is, a student's knowledge is primary, while a student's politics is used in much the same way as we use the comments section on our report cards in the United States — for filler and background information.

Postgraduate Education

China's stated emphasis on advanced scientific and technological education led to our frequent discussion of graduate education admission policies. As we had found in the collegiate selection process, the emphasis at this level as well is on recruiting quality students, that is, students of exceptional intellectual ability. On the several occasions our delegation acted as resource persons in seminars held for the benefit of local educators, an important element of the questioning from the Chinese involved the methods we use in the United States to identify talented students and to draw them into advanced academic training. We noted that in this respect the Chinese and American systems are very similar: both identify the best students in undergraduate programs and then recruit them to go on to advanced programs of research and study.

There are ostensibly three main qualifications for entry into what China calls "postgraduate" education:

1. The student must be a university graduate.

2. The student must have demonstrated an ability to do research.
3. During undergraduate study the student must have shown the stamina to complete a rigorous program of graduate study.

Our impression, however, was that recruitment for postgraduate study is not as systematic as it might seem to be, and by no means is it as clear-cut as the processes of admissions at lower levels. It seemed to us in fact that individual professors are of greatest importance in selecting students for advanced study. Students who perform well in college are simply selected by their individual professors to continue their education and training. All they need do is apply; acceptance is automatic. Political attitudes are assumed to be reliable enough to obviate the need for formal evaluations between the undergraduate and postgraduate years. Similarly, no academic examination is given to ensure scholarly aptitude. At this highest level of education in China, then, admissions policies for all intents and purposes are divorced from politics.

In conclusion, our information concerning the admissions process is based almost exclusively on how Chinese educators thought things should and would work. There was some experimentation in exams occurring while we were in Canton; but virtually no procedure had been fully decided upon, let alone instituted, by the time we left China. The question of whether the system is performing according to the high expectations laid out for us by Minister Liu and his colleagues will have to wait for another delegation.

WORK AND STUDY

Calvin M. Frazier

Commissioner of Education, Colorado

Wilson Riles

Commissioner of Education, California

Within twenty-four hours after our arrival in Peking, all of us became aware of the primacy of the "socialist work ethic" in China's developmental effort. The message came via the loudspeakers on the street corner, the signs on the primary-school playground, and our observations of the students' "production time" in their first grade classes. The impact was clear. One's attitude toward work and his or her specific contributions to group projects were regarded as a key indicator of the individual's loyalty and patriotism.

Article 10 of the Constitution of the People's Republic of China (adopted on March 5, 1978, by the Fifth National People's Congress at its first session) proclaimed the socialist work ethic succinctly and without equivocation.

The state applies the socialist principles: "He who does not work, neither shall he eat" and "from each according to his ability, to each according to his work."

Work is an honorable duty for every citizen able to work. The state promotes socialist labor emulation, and, putting proletarian politics in command, it applies the policy of combining moral encouragement with material reward, with the stress on the former, in order to heighten the citizens' socialist enthusiasm and creativeness in work.

As our visit progressed, formal discussions of pedagogy and less-structured interactions with our hosts and guides enabled us to develop some understanding of the theoretical basis for the combination of work and study in the Chinese curriculum. During an afternoon walk along Shanghai's Bund we discussed the place of the individual and individualism in Chinese society. Our guide, a leading member of the Shanghai education bureau, noted the importance of individual development but stated further that the individual life has worth only in the larger context of group cooperation in the building of socialism to strengthen the nation. This cadre also affirmed his belief that individual development occurs most fully when one engages in productive labor. To produce is to affirm oneself in the material world and thereby to enjoy experiences that nurture the emergence of the personality. Participation in productive labor therefore is essential to the development of socialist consciousness. As our companion warmed to his subject, he tried to help us to understand why in China, for students and intellectuals at least, participation in productive labor is usually equated with manual labor. All productive labor is valuable in socialist education, but students and intellectuals, because of their preoccupation with books and theoretical knowledge, stand in danger of feeling that mental labor is more valuable than is manual labor. Once this seed is planted, said our host, intellectuals and students become arrogant and "divorced from the masses." They develop a false consciousness that does not serve socialism. Therefore, manual labor broadly defined, in theory at least, becomes an integral part of the education of each student at every level of the system. The Chinese are expected to respect, if not love, manual labor, for this is the means by which one's life will come to have meaning to oneself and the nation. Labor is the vehicle for relating to those around you in properly socialist ways. Life has value if the individual is serving the proletariat and, in the absence of a visible threat to the survival of China, the means of keeping the "revolutionary spirit" alive.

This conversation, which occurred near the end of our visit, provided us with a post hoc context for the many similar comments we heard elsewhere. For example, during our visit to Nanking Normal College, an institution which trains middle-school teachers, the vice-chairman of the revolutionary committee began the briefing by informing us that the guiding principle in running the school follows the principle of Chairman Mao, which is "to make education serve proletarian politics and be combined with productive labor, to enable students to develop morally, intellectually, and physically and be trained as workers with both socialist consciousness and culture." In order to carry out this mission, Nanking Normal College operates both a factory and a farm.

By participation in productive labor in these units, the vice chairman assured us that future teachers not only develop their individual consciousness but also combine theory with practice to better learn their coursework. This, he said, better prepares them for their role as teachers. He also told us that the constant experience in productive labor reinforces and underscores official expectations for their subsequent performance in the classroom. Labor participation is a means of defining the mission of teachers.

Our understanding of the principle that participation in productive labor provides meaning for individual development facilitated our coming to terms with the assertion, heard so often, that teachers must develop students who have both the proper political orientation and expertise to contribute to society. That is, that students must be both "red and expert." At Shanghai's No. 2 Middle School we learned that teachers participating in "professional development" sessions were judged by their peers on how well they designed their lessons to give students practical, day-to-day examples in the classroom or during field experiences. We were told many times of the errors of the intellectuals and teachers in trying to tell students about electric motors or the crops to be raised in the surrounding fields with no attempt to have the students experience the lessons through first-hand practical contact. Later, as we strolled through the school grounds one of our interpreters pointed out the inefficacy of stressing work and application at the expense of theory. This he told us was one of the most serious errors of the Gang of Four who had attempted to eliminate the component of theory

from the theory/practice equation. These remarks led us to
conclude that, in the context of Chinese education, work by itself is of little value; it must grow out of and be related to the
substantive and political lessons of the classroom. The ideal
is for students to learn by doing. In the United States a controversy over pedagogical method might be considered a matter of
professional judgment. In China teaching without directly involving the students in productive labor whenever possible becomes a major ideological error.

Work and Study in Kindergarten and Primary School

Our first impression, confirmed by later observations, was
that the central importance of productive work is taught at an
early age. At the No. 2 Peking Kindergarten of the Chung Wen
District a group of four- and five-year-olds entertained us with
a song entitled "We're Brave Little Pilots." This, the kindergarten's director told us, was an example of song designed to
give very young children an awareness of the desirability of
serving the people and the nation. Other songs celebrated and
dramatized the tasks of plowing, planting, and harvesting rice,
while still other selections described the role of different kinds
of workers in the Taching Oilfield Complex. Our interpreter
informed us that these songs were aimed at building an awareness of the importance of agriculture and industry to China's
development, but more importantly, they also sought to make
the students aware of the fact that it was people like themselves
who actually produced these vital goods by the sweat of their
brow, by their exertion in the process of labor. The songs were
in fact a celebration of work. Finally they represent both an
important part of the vocabulary of young children and their
most important role models.

The process of familiarizing students with the habits of discipline, concentration, and mutual interdependence that are associated with modern methods of mass production also begin in
China at an early age. In the No. 2 Peking Kindergarten we observed four- and five-year-olds in a crafts class. The children

were weaving strips of brightly colored paper into attractive belt-like streamers which could be used for decorative purposes. Some children cut the strips of paper, under the careful supervision of a teacher, while others did the actual braiding. A third group tied the ends together to prevent unraveling. We were told that the children did different jobs at different times and that the division of labor that we were observing was not at all permanent. The explanation of this exercise, which was later reinforced by our interpreter, was that in addition to cultivating an appreciation for interesting color patterns, it also required the students to focus attention on one task for a definite period, that it taught them to work cooperatively, and that it enabled the teacher to relate success in achieving goals to such traits as concentration and cooperation. Of course, such traits are applicable in other life situations and the crafts class has many other relevant socializing functions, but it struck us as being significant that the kindergarten director, the teachers, and our interpreter proudly explained their value in terms of building personality traits and habits that would better prepare students for a life of productive labor.

As the Chinese student progresses upward through the grades, symbolic or ritualized exposure to the concept of the centrality of work continues. At the same time, however, he or she also receives increasingly more "realistic" training and experience. This is illustrated by several observations we made in different primary schools, middle schools, and in colleges and universities. For example, first graders in the Peking No. 1 Experimental Primary School, and students from other grades as well, spent several hours each week folding and gluing small cardboard boxes to contain the voice mechanism for the talking dolls produced by a neighborhood toy factory. The school's staff informed us that such activity was considered to be an integral part of the students' education and that accordingly no remuneration was received either by them or by the school. The students worked in a converted classroom, with slogans on its walls that proclaimed the importance of work. Even at the first-grade level students were enjoined to "grasp production" and "go all out to achieve better results." The students spent one 50-minute period each week at this work. It was interesting to note that the atmosphere in the "factory" was well focused and extremely serious. The students seemed to feel that they were doing something they considered to be important. There was little talking except to ask for glue, more pieces of cardboard, or to ask that completed boxes be collected. When we asked to inspect the work, students responded with pride and one told us that his group had in fact exceeded the expected "norms" of production. It was also explained that members of the Little Red Soldiers would take the lead in this activity.

When we asked for a specific statement of how this work was an integral part of the education of each student, different members of the teaching staff were eager to respond. First, they said, this participation enabled young students to develop concrete notions of what it was like to make something in a systematic way. They pointed with some pride to the fact that the converted classroom was organized very much like a regular factory and that the students were in fact producing something of concrete value. Thus we concluded that the experience in effect was intended to simulate in so far as it was possible the atmosphere of a factory so that students could enjoy something of the perceptions of real workers in the real world. Second, the teachers noted that the act of folding and gluing called for the development of manual dexterity, a fact that was of physical benefit to the students and one which also made them more useful later. Third, the teachers informed us that labor participation cultivated those qualities of concentration, self-discipline, and paying attention to the quality of the finished product that were noted earlier with respect to the crafts class of the kindergarten we visited. Most important of all, however, was the assertion that such participation enabled the student to identify in concrete ways with the proletariat who performed such labor on a full-time and regular basis. In this way, students begin to develop, we were told, an appreciation for the reality of the daily lives of the workers and are thereby rendered less susceptible to becoming divorced from labor and from the masses.

A similar mode of participation was described at Hangchow's An-chi-lu Primary School near West Lake in Chekiang Province. Although it was closed down owing to "mechanical problems" during our visit, we saw evidence of the operation of a small but realistic production line in which students filled and labeled small bottles of tincture of iodine. In this case the operation was much more elaborate than was its counterpart in Peking, and we were told that the students spent more time there than one period per week. In fact, the teachers reported that at certain times during the year whole classes manned the line for a week at a time as part of the regular rotation between factory work, farm work, and elementary military training. Despite the difference in scale, however, the intent and purpose of the exercise was essentially identical to all of those we saw during our visit. It was intended to expose students to at least a portion of the environment of the worker by turning them into workers. By acting as a worker, the teachers informed us, a student is supposed to come to think as a worker and to carry that thought pattern throughout his life, whether he winds up in a factory or in a research institute. Later, in conversation with local administrators at Running Tiger Spring, we asked how meaningful such activities could really be since neither the students nor the school received compensation. We also cited the possibility that many students might see such activity as something of a lark or as something to be gotten through in order to achieve other goals. It did seem to us, after all, that despite the attempt to simulate the atmosphere of the factory, the school factories in Peking and Hangchow were in fact rather insulated from the reality of worker life. Those we observed were quite serious about their activities.

Our hosts admitted that patterns of irresponsible behavior did in fact occur and that they were not all that rare. However, it was also reported that teachers, more progressive students such as those in the Little Red Soldiers, and the workers who supervised the factory were all on the alert for evidence of such behavior and that it was taken very seriously by the school staff. We concluded that in Hangchow at least, labor participation involves more than simply playing at work for a short time each year; rather, the resources of the school are mobilized to ensure that the educational function of labor experience is fulfilled. We learned that to this end there are frequent discussions of why students should work; further, students were also encouraged to state their reactions to such activities. Thus, while the aim of labor participation at the primary level appeared to be educational rather than economic, it did in our estimation appear to receive the same seriousness and attention paid to classes in geography, mathematics, and other more traditionally academic subjects. We were not able to view such operations in other primary schools and we therefore refrain from making any broad generalizations concerning either the scope or the intensity of such programs. However, if our observations in Peking, Shanghai, and Hangchow are at all typical even of just urban schools, we can conclude that in China labor forms a dynamic component of the educational experience of the Chinese primary-school student.

As noted above, despite the introduction of actual participation in labor at the primary level, training in the symbols of the importance of labor in both the urban and rural environments also continues. For example, we observed second-grade students doing a unit on agricultural production. The exercise, which lasted for about 50 minutes, involved a diagram of a pig, a model of a tractor, and one of a pump. As the teacher pointed to the different parts of the pig the students were called upon to state the uses of each, apart from food. They also answered questions concerning how pigs are born and how much it costs to raise one. The teacher then asked what the farmers of the Tachai model commune had contributed to the store of knowledge about the raising of pigs. Students responded according to a pattern that seemed to us to be rather set and which emphasized the experimentation and innovation that the members of the Tachai Commune had utilized. The message seemed to be to point up the importance of the peasantry as a repository of a scientific world view that enabled them to make ever increasing contributions to China's development. In this way, we were told, students learn not only about the raising of pigs and their use but also about the value of agricultural labor. By linking Tachai Commune with the advances in animal husbandry, students see the peasants as positive role models and, theoretically at least, cease to distinguish between the value of intellectual and peasant labor.

In the same way, the discussion of how a tractor works was linked to the evolution of improvements that were made in response to problems encountered in plowing. Again students emphasized that it was the peasants who suggested modifications of tractor design and who frequently made them on their own initiative. By asking students to study the evolution of the tractor, teachers repeated the process of underscoring the worth of the peasant and the peasant lifestyle. The unit concluded with a discussion and question-and-answer session on the importance of the pump to the people's communes. Students were expected to respond to questions concerning comparisons of yields before and after the introduction of the pump on a typical commune. There were also questions about the operation of the pump and why its installation was so important. As might be expected, the answers focused upon the utility of the pump in increasing agricultural production. By this method, we learned, students received some idea of the monetary and labor cost attached to producing certain quantities of foodstuffs. This in turn was intended to enable them to manifest an appreciation of the effort and energy that went into the production of their daily food and thereby to gain respect for the necessity of working to improve methods of production. On the basis of these observations we concluded that education and work are closely related at the kindergarten and primary levels, not only through instruction of students on the importance of labor in general but also through actual participation by young children in concrete productive activity.

Work and Study in China's Middle Schools

At the middle-school level the relationship between work and study is essentially similar to that which obtains in China's primary schools. However, there are differences in the quality of the experience and in its intensity. Also, we observed that the goals of such programs became more sophisticated.

In fact, some middle schools utilized what to us seemed a rather unique approach to unifying work and study. The Nanking Technical Power School typified this method. Run by the Ministry of Petrochemicals, this upper middle school (senior high school) trains electricians. Students were of two types. The largest number were graduates of "regular" lower middle schools who had shown an interest in becoming electrical technicians. Accordingly they had been tapped by the officials of these units and enrolled in the regular three-year program. We were not able to gather specific information about how this process of "tapping" had occurred but we were told that they had been "recommended" by lower units.

A second category of students included those who had had several years of practical experience working in factories run by the Ministry of Petrochemicals and who may or may not have ever attended or graduated from lower middle school. These were workers who had demonstrated both an interest in and an aptitude for becoming electrical technicians. These students attended the school for a three-month short course designed to enable them to fill the gaps in their knowledge of mathematics, physics, and the like and also to acquire knowledge of the construction and maintenance of electrical machinery such as generators, transformers, and switch panels. School officials informed us that these students were selected by the cadres and workers of their respective factories to enroll in these short courses.

Finally, the vice-chairman of the school's revolutionary committee told us that the overwhelming majority of the teachers were individuals who had had more than a few years experience as workers in different sorts of factories. He described to us the benefits of this arrangement in the following terms. First he noted that the specialized character of the school and its curriculum facilitated the training of the largest possible number of technicians within a short period of time. Second, and more important from the point of view of inculcating attitudes about work, the school administrators noted that the heterogeneity of the student body resulted in an "evening out" of the attitudes and approaches of the different students. Students with practical work experience tended to be older and more settled. In the judgment of the school staff, they brought with them the outlook and values of the industrial worker. The same characterization was made of the teaching staff. These factors, the vice-chairman said, enabled the younger students to express their more thorough academic preparation in ways that helped the older students while, owing to the differential in age and experience, the younger group was prevented from developing feelings of self-importance. The school staff felt that they had created an environment in which younger people with better training could share that experience with those who had been less fortunate and at the same time acquire the skills, attitudes, and behavior patterns of workers that were so desirable from the political and ideological points of view. The mutual exchange raised cultural levels and inculcated the socialist work ethic.

The school also used work experience as a pedagogical tool. All students were required to spend "several hours each week" in the school-operated factory, which produced electric motors, switchboards, meters, transformers, and other instruments. This experience, the vice-chairman told us, enabled students to relate the theory of the classroom to the practice of the factory floor. While we were unable to determine the exact amount of time spent in this activity, we were assured that it was substantial. Also, as we toured the factory we saw many individuals who clearly were students engaged in various tasks. Their obvious familiarity with the factory environment and with their particular jobs indicated to us that work on the factory floor was in fact a regular practice.

The chairman provided a final example of how his school used practical work experience to reinforce the theoretical knowledge of the classroom when he described the policy of "open-door" schooling enunciated by Mao Tse-tung. Under these precepts, before they can graduate, students are required to go out to other factories to perform productive work such as maintaining and repairing machinery and equipment. It is believed that this work enables the student to work independently, to learn to solve problems, to apply theoretical knowledge, and to enjoy a close interaction with an environment that is similar to that which he or she will soon enter as a contributing member.

The special relationship with the Ministry of Petrochemicals and the specific nature of its mission differentiated the Nanking Technical Power School from other upper middle schools. We have no way of knowing how many schools of this type exist nationally. However, we were impressed by the fact that the Chinese were willing to invest so much energy and resources into ensuring that students received an opportunity to relate their classroom-acquired theoretical knowledge to real-life situations. We also felt that the program and practices of the school illustrated how work itself can be used to inculcate certain attitudes about the value of work. That is, we feel that we saw one important illustration of how our Chinese colleagues attempt to relate theory to practice in developing education.

We were extremely interested to learn that in China work experience seems to be a way of continuing the stress on the liberation of women from traditional roles of subservience. While this can also be said of our observations of primary schools, it seemed to be much more explicit at the middle-school level and above. For example, in the crafts classes and in the primary schools' "factories" cited above, all of the children were equal in terms of their responsibilities. It was the teacher who provided direction. However, in middle-school work settings, the students took a measure of responsibility for their own direction. Although the teacher or supervisor provided overall direction, certain students performed relatively more complex functions than did others. Observations in Nanking, Shanghai, Yangchow, and Hangchow all confirmed an impression that key labor assignments were made without regard to sex differences. Boys and girls all assumed generally equal work roles whether they involved wiring large electric switch panels, constructing a pump, or learning about the operation of a generator. It seems clear that boys and girls are taught essentially the same things and that they are expected to perform such tasks after graduation. This behavior is nurtured from an early age by assigning work roles in ways that do not consider sex. In effect, by placing females in equal roles in what is considered to be the most important context within Chinese society — the workplace — the Chinese attempt to strengthen the concept of equality between the sexes. Equality in work signals equality in other areas.

Another difference between the primary-school and the middle-school experience is seen in the fact that all of the middle schools we visited either had factories on the school grounds or were associated with neighborhood factories and communes in the suburbs. While generalization is difficult, at Shanghai's No. 2 Middle School we learned that students spent about one week each term working in the school factory. However, in this school, assignment to the factory seemed to be correlated with the courses in which the students were enrolled. Students in physics, mathematics, and chemistry courses were most in evidence in the factory while students who had not reached that point in the normal process of course rotation seemed to spend their labor time in the commune's fields. In both cases the object of the labor participation followed the prescriptions noted earlier: students were to have an opportunity to test classroom knowledge in the context of real-life work situations and at the same time to come into intimate contact with less-educated members of society in order to gain first-hand knowledge of their ways of thinking and general world view. The theory as explained to us was that real learning occurs by doing and that this would forestall the development of feelings of elitism.

The Transfer of Urban Youth to the Countryside

Near the end of the Cultural Revolution, in 1966, the Chinese began a program of resettling urban lower- and upper-middle-school graduates on the country's rural and suburban communes. This work program had multiple goals in that urban students received work experience, aided production, and gained a better understanding of the needs of nonurban China. Similarly, we were told by one of our interpreters, the nonurban areas and population benefited from the introduction of a literate and relatively sophisticated group of new residents. In effect, the cultural gap between city and countryside would be narrowed. We learned that this important program had been based on the assumption that the youths would remain in the nonurban setting for life; even if they left their villages to attend college or university, they were expected to return. During the time of our visit, however, it was announced that young people who had been in residence in the countryside for a minimum of two years would be eligible to apply to take the college admission examination. Thus we arrived at a time when the very nature of the transfer seemed to be undergoing a basic redefinition. We had been told before we went to China that this program had caused discontent among many young people because few students were chosen for further study or for alternative kinds of employment and for many this became a permanent exile to the countryside.

As we flew from Shanghai to Canton one evening, the same interpreter who had discussed the transfer program with us earlier became quite irritated with some of us. He stated with some exasperation his feeling that our questions about the transfer program focused excessively upon those students who defied the requirement of work in the countryside and returned to the cities. He told us that he had read such stories in the Western press and found the accounts to be greatly exaggerated. He admitted that a few students had returned illegally to the cities but their numbers, he said, were infinitesimal.

We were never really able to resolve this question to our own satisfaction. The only students we were able to contact were those who had been in the countryside and who had returned legally to the cities to become university students and those who were still in upper middle school and not yet faced with the prospect of spending time with the peasants. Nonetheless, when we asked members of both groups what they thought of either the experience or the prospect, they responded that they were glad to have served or that they would be glad to serve the country in this way. We felt that we had received a set response from these youth. However, when we asked similar questions of parents the responses varied.

In Shanghai, one rather highly placed parent told us that she was entirely accepting of the program of "sending down" and felt it to be both a duty and a privilege for her son to have such an opportunity to serve. In fact, she stated that she felt a certain pride in the fact that her son had been sent to Inner Mongolia and that even after he had been permitted to return to Shanghai to receive a college education, he chose to resume his work in that remote area. At the same time, another mother we interviewed expressed grave misgivings about the possibility of her children being sent down. She was afraid that they might never be able to return and frankly admitted to feeling that they could make a greater contribution to the revolution by receiving advanced education and then by working in the cities. Finally, still another mother said very honestly that she hoped her son could pass the necessary examinations and go directly to college in order to avoid being sent down. It was clear that she believed the transfer program at times resulted in a waste of talent.

It seemed to us that the whole program of transfer was in a state of transition or at least that it was on the verge of being redefined. Most officials with whom we spoke seemed pleased at the prospect of changes in the program. Further, we sensed that many cadres did regard the transfer program as arbitrary in its application, thereby depriving many deserving young people of the chance to develop intellectual and other skills.

This impression was reinforced in subsequent observations. We sensed discontent not only among parents and youth but also among leaders who had worked with the program in a "receiving commune" just outside of Shanghai. We were told by a commune spokesman that over the past years 300 of 500 youth sent to the commune had remained. Since selection for college is very restricted, it can be assumed that only a few of the 200 youth returning to the city went back to higher education assignments.

On what basis the remainder of the 200 had returned was left unclear, but the mere fact of the departure of so large a number indicates that there are many routes back to the cities.

It was our impression that the transfer program was receiving increasingly less emphasis. College and university entrance requirements were being reevaluated, and in Hangchow we were told that this would result in a modification of the two-year work requirement. Some students were to be allowed to go directly from middle school to college on grounds that a two-year break in certain subject areas such as mathematics and science would be detrimental to the development of a cadre of trained personnel in these important areas. Thus, our tentative conclusion is that this interesting and unique attempt to link work with the process of social and moral-political education is being reexamined and that the future will probably bring about basic changes in both the scope and intensity of the transfer program.

Work and Study in Colleges and Universities

The relationship between work and study at the highest levels of the educational ladder represent the logical extension of the relationship at the middle levels. The experience is more systematic. In some ways it is also less intense, since students enrolled in colleges during the time of our visit all had done at least two years in labor assignments before enrolling. As at the middle-school level, labor assignments seemed to be tied to specific specializations or majors. At Peking Normal University, for example, students in the sciences worked in the school-run factory that produced transistors. Other students in the nonscientific fields, we were told, worked on the university-run farm which was integrated into a commune on the outskirts of Peking. Conversations with students at Peking Normal revealed a basically positive attitude about labor participation. Several students indicated that they saw such opportunities as providing a welcome break from the normal routine of classes. Most of the students with whom we conversed seemed to feel quite sincerely that such experience was most valuable in developing social and political attitudes. In no case did we receive an impression that labor participation during the school year was something that had to be "endured" in order to progress to something else. Rather, it was viewed as a necessary and valuable part of the individual student's total education.

At every university and, indeed, in every unit we visited we inquired about difficulties in making the labor experience directly relevant to course work. In no case did we receive a satisfactory answer. Our impression was that our counterparts had settled for a compromise of sorts in which they recognized that a direct connection between courses and labor was impossible to achieve in every case and that when this occurred, the function of labor was to offer a supplement to substantive education. What they did see as being most important was that labor participation was the core of political and moral education and that it provided the vehicle whereby young people were exposed to alternative modes of thinking and to different sets of social values, which was most consonant with building a socialist society. For example, a professor of physics at Peking Normal University told us that labor was important in the program of his department because it enabled engineers to learn to think as members of the proletariat and the peasantry. "It provides a means by which intellectuals come to identify with the masses of workers and peasants and thereby enables education to serve proletarian politics."

Conclusion

Clearly our time in China was insufficient to enable us to develop a definitive assessment of the relationship between work and study in the Chinese curriculum. Our information is sketchy and was derived in rather piecemeal fashion. However, we left China convinced that participation in productive labor is viewed as an invaluable pedagogical tool both in enriching the classroom experience and especially in inculcating attitudes related to individual social-political development. Labor becomes the means by which notions of the collective good and the basic value of many different types of effort are illustrated for China's young people. We are also confident in stating that this approach to education will continue despite the recent dramatic changes in the educational system.

There are, however, certain questions. Our conversations with teachers, students, administrators, and Party members all indicated that there is relatively less agreement concerning the optimum mix of labor and intellectual substance in the total educational experience of the individual student. We were made aware of the existence of strong pressures to tap bright students and to develop them along substantive lines. It seems to us that this cannot but qualify the importance of work in the educational process. Our hosts seemed to feel that they were faced with a zero-sum game in which time devoted to labor was time taken away from formal study of academic subjects. Thus, our Chinese colleagues seemed to be most concerned with working out a formula that would enable the combination of the two components in a utilitarian manner. In any case and whatever the ultimate resolution, in China work and study have been integrated to a degree unsurpassed elsewhere in the world.

EARLY CHILDHOOD EDUCATION

*Lillian Weber**

Director of the Workshop Center for Open Education

Three factors influenced our observations of early childhood education in China. First, "education" in China conveys a meaning that transcends the interactions that occur in the classroom. As we heard during our formal interview with the Minister of Education, education is an integral aspect of the process of revolutionary social change and, since social change requires mass involvement, all environments in effect become learning environments. Schools are but one element of the learning space that is the larger society.

Second, our delegation was made up of educational administrators. Because they were aware of this, our hosts quite understandably arranged a program of visits designed to afford us an overview of the entire educational system. We did not and could not concentrate on the formal areas of early childhood education — nurseries, kindergartens, and the lower levels of the primary schools — and we were able to visit only four kindergartens and three primary schools before leaving China. As we came to accept the primacy of family relationships and environmental surroundings in the education of young children, we found that our observations became oriented toward the total context of childhood life rather than toward the limited area of activities within the school itself. In many respects the streets became a most important source for understanding early childhood education; what we saw of children and families on our visits to tourist sites, communes, department stores, railroad stations, restaurants, and other places added immeasurably to our experience.

Third, because our interpreter-escorts were parents as well as representatives of the Ministry of Education, they too became a source of understanding for us. As we rode together on trains and buses, they answered questions from their experiences as children growing up in China and as parents themselves. These conversations also provided a context for observations made elsewhere in more formal educational situations. For example, one of our escorts told us how his son, a second grader, had applied what he had learned about freezing in his school's "common knowledge" class; the child had wrapped the family goldfish in cloth to keep them warm during the harsh Peking winter!

In retrospect it seems impossible to recollect any scene in China that does not include children. They are as much a feature of the landscape as are the photographs of Mao Tse-tung. We were most impressed by the air of easy acceptance that characterizes the relations between children and adults. One day, while strolling in Peking's Tien An Men Square, our attention was drawn by the fact that nearly all of the groups around us included children. It was our impression that children are naturally and unselfconsciously included in family events outside the home. In several groups we observed males (probably the fathers) carrying children on their shoulders. At no time did we feel that adults regretted the presence of children nor did we see any manifestations of impatience or scolding. Children seem not to be excluded from the adult world; rather, they appear to be carried along into it as if they were small adults. Parents apparently expect to share their experiences with their children and the children in turn seem to react to these expectations in an easy, accepting, and remarkably adult-like manner.

We were similarly impressed by the ready gentleness with which children relate to each other in China. While walking along the Bund in Shanghai, we noticed a group of boys and girls of early primary-school age pause at a corner to cross a busy street. Several children expressed concern for the safety of the group. No child was allowed to cross without several others watching for cars and shouting when it was safe and when it was not, and several children took the hand or arm of the child nearest them to cross the intersection in tandem. The fact that our conversations with teachers indicated that all Chinese children are taught the rules of traffic safety does not fully explain the ease and spontaneity that characterized this interaction.

Part of this openness among the children may be due to the fact that Chinese youngsters seem to have ample opportunity for unsupervised, spontaneous play. Our hotel rooms in Shanghai opened on a residential neighborhood where each morning and afternoon, before and after school hours, we saw numerous instances of boys engaged in casual soccer games and groups of young girls taking turns jumping rope. This led us to observe that despite China's crowded conditions, it is possible for Chinese children to be part of a large group and still be comfortable and preserve one's private space. Outside of the structured environment offered by home, kindergarten, nursery, or school, children can and do create their own environments for play in an essentially spontaneous manner. Adults seem to expect this of children and treat such behavior as a matter of course. As one of our interpreters remarked, children's games are broken up only if the activity poses a threat to their safety.

The air of cooperation, acceptance, and mutual responsibility was maintained even in situations where normal expectations break down: when two individuals had differences, the group would respond with cooperation and a feeling of responsibility. As we arrived in the Shanghai railroad station we happened on an incident in which an adult male was restrained from punching a policeman who had accused the man of stealing a bicycle. In this instance, as in every other case of difference of opinion we saw, the onlookers and bystanders participated in a clear group effort to achieve a solution. It was not totally surprising for us, therefore, to witness the same kind of free and easy group cooperation even among preschool children. The educative context in which the children of China grow up involves a moral imperative to commit themselves to the concepts of cooperative assistance and mutual benefit and to reveal this commitment in their personal actions. Chinese educators and propagandists alike succinctly describe this educative context as a commitment to the ideal of "Serve the People."

The impressions reported above are based upon observations of young children behaving in essentially informal and unstructured situations. Of course this picture is incomplete. Much of a child's time is spent in environments in which structure is extremely important. What did observations of schools, kindergartens, and nurseries tell us about different aspects of early childhood education in China?

School Observations

The dominant impression reflected in the reports of previous delegations is that rote learning is the major characteristic of Chinese school methodology. Generally speaking, our own observations confirm this impression. However, we also noted numerous examples of nonrote methods. We saw more than a few instances in which the child was allowed to interact directly with the material or learning situation rather than required to follow strictly in a path set by the teacher. Of course, some situations and materials lend themselves naturally to such direct encounter.

In fact this question of rote and nonrote teaching methodology became a topic of lively discussion between ourselves and our Chinese counterparts. It also provided a subject for discussion during the hours when members of our group gathered for informal comparison of notes and impressions at the end of the day. Ultimately we concluded that part of the reason for our own inability to agree on the relative place of rote vs. nonrote methods arose from the fact that we frequently use the word "rote" as though it were synonymous with "whole class." We further agreed that it might increase the utility of our observations if we were to separate from "whole class" our concept of "rote" and "unison." In rote and unison lessons the whole class is involved, but responsively, whereas when a whole class is doing something in response to teacher demand and focus, differences in pace and timing tend to become marked. The reasons for whole-class presentation are not the same as the purposes served by unison responses, and neither method of organization may serve other needs, such as the need for practice or experience with materials in learning, or provide for response to individual need. Thus, we concluded that while much learning in the Chinese classroom is in fact rote, there are also a large number of whole class experiences that do provide for some measure of individual initiative and response.

In this context we observed that in mathematics the idea of the primacy of rote methods requires some qualification. At Peking's No. 1 Experimental Primary School we observed that second graders were required to manipulate certain concrete materials as they progressed through the lesson. In the case we observed, students were required to confront an abacus and the confrontation was direct and individual and allowed the students to move at individualized speeds. We also saw young members of Peking's No. 2 Kindergarten of the Chung-wen District engaged in direct manipulation of concrete materials as they learned basic numbers. The four- to six-year-old children were required to match such objects as trees and baskets cut from paper with written numerals. This activity also required direct, active engagement and seemed also to permit the individual student to move at his or her own speed. Later, at Hangchow's An-chi-lu Primary School, we observed a mathematics demonstration for a class of older children who were in the fifth grade. Here the teacher explained the principles involved to the whole class, asked for questions, and then repeated the demonstration in the context of a different story problem. The class immediately broke into small groups to solve other problems based upon the same principle. The pattern involved two groups of two children who turned to each other and formed a group of four around a desk. Each group worked more or less independently while the teacher walked about the room, listened to the discussions, and monitored the progress of the class. Each group then was called upon to present its solution and in doing so to explain why it had reached its answer. The teacher then commented upon the propriety of the answer and criticized the announced line of reasoning. Finally, at a primary school on a commune in suburban Canton, one member of our group asked a question about the teaching of additional forms of practical mathematics. The teacher knew immediately what was meant and responded that the students (second graders) would be measuring the school yard that afternoon. These observations of course do not support the conclusion that the teaching of mathematics embraces a wide variety of nonrote methods. Indeed we could cite many examples of unison responses in which engagement with material was less than active and in which only one outcome was possible. However, we do conclude that the teaching of mathematics at least seems to include a variety of rote and nonrote methods.

We also observed marked variations in the teaching of art. At the No. 2 Experimental Primary School in Peking we saw first and second graders coloring-in outline drawings. There was little room for individual expression in this exercise, leading several of us to wonder whether or not the teacher wanted the students to see the relationships between the particular colors that were prescribed. Incidentally, all of the members of our group were impressed by the fine quality and careful workmanship evident in the work of each student. However, in another class in the same school we saw students following the teacher as she drew a picture of a blossom-laden branch of a cherry tree. In this case, although the major outlines and stroke orders were established by the teacher, each student seemed free to make variations as he or she saw fit. We noted that the teacher did not seem to treat these rather numerous variations as mistakes or errors. On the contrary, she seemed to encourage them by telling individual students how nice each picture was. Our observation on this point was that the teacher was clearly not trying to have the students draw the same picture. Rather, she was presenting a general lesson on perspective and spatial relationships and allowing each student to express himself within these limits. In Shanghai and Hangchow we saw five-year-olds engaged in free drawing. In each case we noted a fineness of background detail that led us to conclude that the teacher had in fact encouraged it by asking each student to discuss his or her individual observations. We felt that she had asked each student, "What do you see?" and "What might be there?" Similarly, in the Shanghai Children's Palace we saw a large and impressive display of the artwork of students of different ages. In each case the differences in detail, subject matter, manner of execution, brush/pen technique, and choice of colors indicated a wide latitude for personal expression by the individual student. Finally, among the very young children in kindergartens we visited we saw many examples of representational work done in plasticene. The subjects included trucks, automobiles, and people. The detail was quite fine and reflected individual variations from child to child. As with the case of teaching mathematics, we do not conclude from these observations that rote methods are not applied in the teaching of art. Rather, we simply point out that both rote and nonrote methods and techniques seem to have a place in the Chinese repertoire of methods for the teaching of young children.

Another consistent feature of early childhood education is the field trip, particularly in connection with early primary classes in "common knowledge," a subject very much like our own elementary general science. Virtually every unit we visited reported the application of the field trip method in this area and it was clear that children were encouraged to report their observations in an individual manner. As we listened to a third-grade class in Peking discuss a recent series of observations, it was clear that the students had not been programmed to see similar sets of things. The teacher accepted each observation reported, commented on it, and asked the student to relate it to what had been learned in the class prior to the trip. As the lesson drew to a close, the teacher then summarized the observations and made a kind of general presentation to the whole class. Of course, such a subject as "common knowledge" lends itself quite readily to direct engagement and it is in this area that there is probably the greatest room for individual expression and application of creative thought.

It was in the general area of language learning that the mixture of rote and nonrote methods seemed to us to be most apparent. In the primary grades, the common practice seemed to call for the teacher to write a series of characters on the board and then to call upon the class to recite them. This process was repeated over and over for each character, with the students changing the responses in a high elocutionary style of voice. We encountered this style of voice whenever recitation was called for in all of our visits and it seems designed to provide maximum clarity in a country where regional variations in pronunciation are so marked as to present a problem of major proportions. The teacher would then call upon each student in turn to use the character presented in a sentence. As noted elsewhere in this report, the examples chosen by students usually reflected what we felt to be rather set responses that embodied political and moral precepts current at the time. We also observed that rote methods seemed to prevail in the teaching of reading and writing. Students were taught to write characters in a particular order of strikes and there was no room for variation. Finally, in reading, students all read together. It seemed to us that in the primary grades and above, rote methods seem to predominate in the area of language teaching. Of course this is at least partially explained by the nature of the Chinese language, which requires memorization, and it is also reasonable to assume that teachers would quite understandably want their students to write characters in approved, standardized ways.

However, with young children, language teaching seems to center upon song, drama, and storytelling. This approach continues through the lower primary grades. In Peking and in Shanghai we observed the preparation of songs, dances, and stories for telling. The process is as follows: Typically, the teacher discusses the song, the dance, or the story, asks the children about what they are dramatizing, and thereby attempts to enrich their understanding of the piece. Then one or two children perform while others watch or sing along as a chorus. Then one or two other children sing or dance the same segment, offering variations in tone, dance movements, or accents. Through this process, different degrees of expressiveness are elicited from the children in ways that seem very much like the methods of American teachers of movement. Children in China are asked to think about how they might express one or another aspect of the story, though the final expression invariably reflects more teacher control than do similar productions in the United States. It was our impression that these exercises have two basic goals. The first is to develop within the kindergarten pupil and the older nursery-schoolchild an awareness and familiarity with basic words, sentence patterns, sounds, and ways of expressing thoughts. This, we felt, accounted for the adherence to the basic lines of the story, song, or dance dramatization. Discussion of the performance between teachers and children enriches the understanding of the subject and at the same time encourages children to experiment with different sounds, tonal patterns, word associations, plays on words, and the like. In this way, it seemed to us, individual children can proceed with language development according to their own individual capacities. They also learn to innovate and to change set patterns within the context of familiar materials.

In concluding these observations it should be clear that rote learning methods are of basic and primary importance in the teaching of young children. However, we did observe that at all levels from kindergarten into the primary grades, there exists a mix of rote and nonrote methods and that as a rule, nonrote methods are frequently more in evidence in the education of preschool children. The child progressing from kindergarten through the primary grades confronts increasingly more rote learning situations.

Teacher Relations with Young Children

The relationship between teachers and young children seems to follow from that which obtains between young children and adults generally. That is, the relationship calls for adaptiveness by adults and responsiveness to the perceived needs of children. Our observations in kindergartens in Peking, Shanghai, and Nanking indicated what is perhaps best described as an interplay of responses. In Nanking we saw a kindergarten teacher lead the children by being responsive to their interests. The teacher had started a circle game and immediately encountered some difficulty: the children wanted to run. The teacher quickly adjusted her focus to set up a running game in which the children participated with enthusiasm. This observation was confirmed elsewhere in different kindergarten settings. Chinese teachers do not seem to decide what is appropriate and then try to convince the children to do what the teacher considers to be best. Rather, teachers attempt to tune into the desires of the children and then to construct an activity consonant with their preferences. We observed very little insisting of any sort.

This adaptiveness of teacher response was also very much in evidence in the one or two nurseries we visited. All of us were impressed by the warm and supportive nature of teacher interaction with very young children. For example, in Hangchow we paid an unannounced visit to a nursery run by a factory that produced silk brocade. In that nursery, as in others that we saw, a child would be picked up and comforted if it started to cry or would not sleep. During our visit most of the infants and toddlers were asleep, but two children were in the arms of caretakers while two others were sitting in chairs holding toys. The caretakers informed us that "they wouldn't sleep so, rather than insist, we picked them up." In a nursery in Shanghai two three-year-old children started to cry when a nurse-teacher started to demonstrate a wind-up toy. Rather than remonstrating with them, one of the caretakers simply picked them up, cuddled them, and laughed with them until they were reconciled to the situation. In sum, the relationship between the teacher and the very young child seems to be one in which the teacher acts as a supporter whose job it is to respond to child-expressed needs and to achieve educational goals by taking advantage of the needs of the children at the time they express their needs.

Early childhood education in China involves an interplay between rote and nonrote methods of teaching and relating to children, with the component of rote methods increasing as the child matures. Also, the education of young children in China involves a view of the teacher as an individual who accepts the preferences of children and who matches these preferences to a wide repertoire of pedagogical devices to achieve certain desired results. Young children are accepted for what they are and adults seem to feel that they can learn best if they are responded to in terms that reflect their particular needs at particular times. As the child grows older, there is concomitantly more directiveness, and eventually it seems to be the child who does more of the adapting. In other words, as childhood comes to an end, and it seems to end rather early, the individual confronts a learning environment that is more structured and requires that he or she adapt to its requirements.

FAMILY AND COMMUNITY INVOLVEMENT

Grace C. Baisinger

President, National Parent-Teachers Association

Virginia Macy

President, California Parent-Teachers Association

Virtually every adult we met in China was a parent with a child in school. Thus, while the number of households we visited was small, we had many conversations centering on parenthood, the role of elders, and the problems associated with raising children. Although our discussions revealed that parents, grandparents, and members of the community all play a large part in the overall education of China's children, we were interested in the fact that these same individuals do not have a significant influence on the formal education their children receive inside the classroom. That is to say that members of families and communities govern students' informal, social education as it occurs whenever children are away from school; but their influence on such matters as curriculum, textbook and material selections, and teaching methodology is minimal. Our observations in the areas we toured and of the people we met led us to conclude that parental and community involvement is enlisted by the school system only to the extent this involvement supports the political and moral objectives of the system and that it is not allowed to present suggestions that contradict or attempt to modify what actually goes on in the classroom.

Although each child receives an education from what are essentially two different worlds, one within and one without the classroom, it is also true that each source of instruction is designed to reinforce the other. This can only occur with interaction between the two sources of instruction. The purpose of this chapter, therefore, is to identify the role of family and community in the education of China's students, and to describe the way in which each interacts with the primary source of educational direction in China — the teacher in the classroom.

The Older Generation

In striking contrast to what we are accustomed to in the United States, in China we came across repeated examples of the fact that grandparents enjoy a close and proximate relationship with their grandchildren and, further, that they feel themselves to be more than partially responsible for the rearing and education of the child. In some instances it seemed that the grandparents were even more conscientious than the parents, who were preoccupied with their work.

In the Tsao-yang Workers' Village in Shanghai, the Huang-tu People's Commune in Kiangsu, the Mei-chia-wu Production Brigade in Chekiang, the Jen-he People's Commune in Canton, and in continuing conversations with our hosts and guides, we learned that a common household configuration includes three generations: grandparents, parents, and children. Even in those cases where the grandparents do not actually live in the same room with the rest of the nuclear family, their home or apartment is frequently within a few minutes walk away. Both parents usually work outside the home; often they have different shifts, which reduces their time not only with each other but with their children. Occasionally the parents are forced by circumstances to reside in different cities, such as the female leader of the Huang-tu Commune near Shanghai whose husband is a merchant seaman homeported in Canton — about 700 miles away. (They manage to see each other only twice a year.) Although it is an unpopular practice, it is apparently not unusual for parents to be separated because of a conflict in their job responsibilities. With the grandparents living at home and the parents either across the country or across town working, the effect is that the role of "parent educator" falls to the grandparents as much by default as by China's long tradition of veneration of the elderly.

Due to the high praise we had heard about China's numerous day-care centers and infant nurseries, we assumed, erroneously perhaps, that these institutions were far more significant in terms of child care in China than any other means. But after a week or so in China we began to change this view, especially when Yang Hsia-yin, revolutionary committee chairman of a commune near Shanghai, made the observation (purely her own estimate) that the largest number of children in China are still cared for in the home by grandparents and that only a minority, maybe even a shrinking minority, of children spend their early days in the care of nonfamily members and surrogate mothers.

Our impression that it is the grandparents who have the most continuous and stable contact with children while they are not in school was reinforced during our visit to the Shanghai Tsaoyang Workers' Village. In one home the family unit consisted of a grandmother, her daughter and son-in-law, and a young girl of four. The mother and father work different shifts in a nearby factory, so it falls to the grandmother to prepare most of the meals, do the daily cleaning, and supervise the behavior of her granddaughter. In another home members of our group who thought they had opened a door to the stairwell exit were surprised and embarrassed to realize they had entered the living quarters of another family in which a pair of grandparents and their granddaughter, an upper middle-school graduate, were just sitting down to a meal. We quickly learned that the granddaughter was about to be married and the grandparents, who had vicariously enjoyed and guided her through courtship, were busily engaged in preparing her for married life by teaching her how to cook, sew, and cope with seasonal variations in food prices, and by advising her what kinds of household appliances and furniture to buy. Instead of moving in with the granddaughter's parents or the new son-in-law's family, the newlyweds — according to the grandparents — were going to move into the apartment we so unexpectedly visited until the new couple could find separate quarters of their own.

Although we were struck by the degree of involvement of the grandparents in bringing up the young, we noted that the substantive educative role of grandparents is less directly concerned with formal education such as it occurs in the classroom than with the kind of social education that is found in person-to-person relationships but not in textbooks. For instance, all the grandparents we met were retired workers, some of whom had completed courses in basic literacy since China's new government came to power in 1949. Predictably, they use this ability to keep themselves posted on the latest political trends, to write letters, and to read stories to young family members. What they do not use their newly developed literacy for, and this again contrasts with the United States where families often advise children on school-related problems, is to help relate the intellectual component of the classroom experience to the child by assisting with homework, projects, experiments, and the like.

Because parents are often physically absent from the Chinese household for long or irregular periods of time, the grandparents also act as the child's principal agents of socialization, teachers of social skills, and models to emulate. To the extent that the older generation spans the gap between the "old" society — before Liberation — and the new, they serve as living examples of the changes that have occurred in China as a result of social revolution under Mao. These factors have combined to give rise to yet another avenue of involvement of grandparents and elders of the Chinese society in China's educational system. All over China, especially in factories but also in school laboratories, we witnessed a number of ways in which China employs intergenerational contact inside the schools, so that the young can learn from the old in a systematic manner. This innovative educational technique ordinarily features a retired member of the community working part- or even full-time in a secondary or post-secondary school as part of the institution's general curriculum on political education. In this regard, one major responsibility of a retired worker in a school is to explain the changes that have occurred in their lives since Liberation by vividly relating to the students the horrors of World War II China and comparing the circumstances then to the relative peace and prosperity of the present. Beyond this political function, however, elders are also asked to teach their practical skills, which as retirees they no longer gainfully use, to young apprentices. It is not unusual, therefore, to enter a Chinese middle school (very few elders work in primary schools) and find a retired worker with no teaching credentials other than life experience, working side-by-side with a student one-fifth his age, teaching the secrets of his acquired practical skills. We did not see, but we were told, that these same elders occasionally describe to the students the bitterness of life in prerevolutionary China. A member of the education department of the Shanghai municipal revolutionary committee told us during a banquet that she and other members of the bureau were trying to define new ways and means of expanding intergenerational contact in schools with the specific intent of conveying the politically profound contrast between "old" and "new" China.

Parents

The participation of parents in their children's education should not be underestimated, however, since it does occur in various fashions and to various degrees. The most intense interaction between the school and the student's home environment, in fact, usually occurs as a result of contact between teachers and parents, rather than between teachers and grandparents.

In most of the schools we visited, teachers informed us that their contacts with parents most often take place as one parent or another delivers or picks up the child at school. Although this practice is more widespread among parents of younger children, since it is a custom for parents to walk their youngsters home from school when conditions permit, it sometimes extends to older children as well. We were told that such contacts involve the exchange of ad hoc bits of information concerning the state of the child's health, performance in class on that particular day, behavior, and news of forthcoming events such as field trips, with which the parents should be concerned. Clearly such interaction must occur in all countries. What distinguishes China from the United States, however, is the fact that Chinese parents and teachers appear to regard such practices as part of their respective formal duties. Virtually all of the primary schools we visited reported a similar pattern of parent-teacher interaction, although they did not specify whether mothers or fathers are more frequently involved.

We also noted a number of other modes of formal interaction between schools and parents. Twice a year, at the beginning and end of the school year, parents are called to general meetings at the school. There they are informed about the general curriculum, the expectations held for the students, and events at which the students must be present, such as dance performances, celebrations of national holidays, and other special events. Sometimes, after the general meeting, parents have individual conferences with the teachers of their children, although such meetings may be skipped by mutual consent if there is no compelling reason to meet or if too many other parents are in line to talk with the teacher. In the case of parents with whom the teacher is familiar and whose child is doing well in academic and political work, this sort of formal conference is rare.

But in the case of a new student or a newly returned parent, conferences are more likely to occur, just as they do in the United States. In China, however, one important difference is seen in the fact that the teachers make it a practice to personally visit the homes of new students and interview the whole family in order to gain background information that will make for an easier relationship between all parties concerned.

Yet another form of regularized communication between parents and teachers occurs through the medium of the student workbook or a special notebook in which messages are sent from the teacher to the student's family. In Hangchow's An-chi-lu Primary School, for example, we learned that comments in the student's workbook are usually directed toward problem areas in particular subjects. Parents are expected to help resolve these problems either by supervising homework or by providing outside tutorial assistance if they can find it. In some schools each student has a special notebook in which teachers regularly write comments concerning general progress and pose questions which the parents are expected to answer. Typical are queries concerning the amount of sleep a student has been getting and questions relating to diet and general deportment. It was interesting to note that teachers and parents alike seem to view this device as one designed to help the student rather than as a mechanism for maintaining discipline, although this would surely be a concomitant of the practice.

Based upon these observations made in some of China's major urban areas we developed the impression that the teachers, particularly at the primary level, possess a commendably intimate knowledge of the background and family circumstances of most of their students and that the development of such knowledge is considered to be an integral aspect of their general duties. Teachers are expected to have such knowledge and parents are expected to provide it.

We had less success in discerning the nature of parental involvement in secondary schools and in both primary and secondary schools in suburban areas. It was our impression that informal contacts are much fewer at the secondary level and above since older students tend to come and go more independently. However, it is clear that parents are invited to and do willingly attend general meetings at which broad topics are discussed. In the suburban communes the nature of the living environment seems to support a pattern of close relations. During our visit to the Shanghai commune, for instance, few students were in evidence around the school since most had been called into service to bring in the autumn harvest. We were also told that most of the teachers were in the fields with them. If this is common practice, and we were told that it is, it seems reasonable to conclude that teachers and students and families all have significant contact outside of the school where opportunities to discuss student progress must present themselves regularly.

Quite often we observed that the nature of parent-teacher relationships, especially at or above the secondary level, is conditioned by the pattern of relations between parents and their offspring. We concluded, moreover, that parent-child relations are undergoing a period of change that could lead to even less parent-teacher interaction than already occurs. We drew this from the feeling we gained in the homes we visited and especially in more detailed conversations with our escorts and local hosts, that there seems to be a gradual erosion of the tradition of defining family functions on the basis of either sex or relationship. Mr. Chi, our interpreter, reported that he and his wife share household tasks according to who is free at the time. This leads him to frequently attend to the tasks of mending, washing clothes, and cooking. With regard to children, Mr. Chi and others explained that young parents in China are attempting to implant and nurture a "critical spirit" in their young children. They are learning to accept and to encourage the practice of having their children "speak out" on matters of family relations. When we restated the comments of our guide in terms of infusing traditional vertical, "parent-over-child" relations of authority with a more horizontal component of "parent-equals-child," thereby increasing family "democracy," he replied that we had phrased it accurately. He also admitted that his parents were having some difficulty adjusting to this concept. Thus, to the extent that our miniscule sample can be extended, it seems that relations between parents and between parents and children in urban China are gradually "evening out."

One manifestation of this trend is reflected in the responses of teachers at different schools to our questions concerning the nature of parental involvement in the educational experience. At the No. 1 Experimental Primary School in Peking (where Mr. Chi's son is a pupil), we were informed that the students themselves are expected to serve as the main carriers of information from the school to their parents and that pupils are taught that this is one of their responsibilities as citizens. More specifically, students are expected to inform their parents of their perception of their own progress and to undertake a self-evaluation of their academic work, political attitude, and general behavior. Similarly, children are expected to report to their teachers on their conduct at home, including the amount of time spent on homework, how they spend their leisure time, and what kinds of help-oriented tasks they perform around the home in line with the requirements of proper citizenship training.

Slow Learners

During the course of every primary and middle school visit, we asked about how the teachers and staff deal with problems of slow-learning pupils or with those students who for some reason emerge as discipline problems. It is clear from the responses of the teachers that students are not viewed as either "fast" or "slow." Rather, they are seen as those who learn easily and those who require some help. Similarly, in terms of conduct, students are not seen as being "good" or "bad," but as being those who behave in acceptable ways and those who require some assistance in adjusting their attitudes. The difference between these two manners of interpreting student behavior is more than semantic. One assumes that the innate abilities of students vary from one student to the next; the other assumes that all students are equally able but, because of circumstances, some need help.

In the Shanghai No. 2 Middle School we asked whether teachers observed problems as students make the transition from childhood into adolescence. We were told that sometimes Chinese youth seem to reflect a sense of rootlessness and inability to focus attention at this age. We were also informed that as students reach puberty, they sometimes become distracted and require special attention. This illustrates our observation that Chinese teachers feel there are always reasons to explain different patterns of behavior and that it is not the patterns which require definition, isolation, and treatment, but rather the root causes. Thus the phrases "errant behavior" and "slow learner" have no solid operational meaning in the context of Chinese education. They describe patterns that are traceable to causes such as the age of the child, the child's diet, home circumstances, relationships with others of the same age, etc.

In line with this, Chinese educators pointed out to us that a student's divergence from normal behavior patterns is an important stimulus for parental interaction with the teacher and the school. If a Chinese student begins to evidence what we in the United States would call either a "learning" problem or a "discipline" problem, Chinese teachers undertake a series of home visits during which they interview both the parents and the student in an attempt to discover the origin of the problem. The origin of the problem must always be found outside the student; it can never be due to something that is internalized. At Nanking Normal College, where a good number of middle-school teachers for Nanking are trained, we learned that apprentice teachers are instructed in the methods of conducting such interviews and that they also learn how to prepare and supervise a program of "remedial" instruction. Such instruction programs involve their own participation along with the parents' efforts and the combined efforts of a few of the lagging student's more secure classmates. There are also cases in which neighbors are called in to provide the support the student needs to overcome his circumstances. Although we were pleased that the teachers we met were able to discuss these questions with us more openly than may have been the case in the past, we were disappointed that we were not able to develop a "case history" to provide an empirical example of this mode of dealing with student problems.

Community Involvement

The question of the role of the community in the affairs of local schools was also of interest to the members of our group. While we encountered a great deal of rhetoric asserting the importance of such involvement, and while it was clear that community organizations of various kinds were active in different areas of school operations, it was difficult to discern the scope of such involvement and the pattern, if any, of interaction.

During a banquet at the Shanghai Mansions overlooking Shanghai harbor, a member of the Municipal Education Department discussed her plans for a city-wide organization of women's groups to become more active in the city's schools. These groups provide education and support for women in their daily lives, as well as an opportunity to discuss with other women problems they are having with their husbands, children, jobs, health, child-raising, women's rights, etc. These organizations also take as an area of concern the operation of their local schools, each member working to organize communication between school officials and parents and discussions concerning special problems the school faces, enlisting "outside assistance" when necessary to solve a problem. In Shanghai it is usually a member of one of these groups who takes the lead in arranging to talk with the parents of a student who is having difficulty in school. In general terms, we gained the impression that these organizations function as a kind of cutting edge for the school administration in communicating with parents and others outside the school. Our host emphasized that this phenomenon has not yet spread beyond the environs of Shanghai and that even in the city it is still only in its formative stages.

Perhaps the greatest involvement of the community at-large in the educational process is seen in the area of extracurricular education. While educators at all levels told us that they did not believe in grouping according to ability, they also recognized that some students do learn more rapidly than others. These students receive special attention by participation in after-school clubs that sponsor model airplane and ship construction and biology and chemistry experiments, to cite some activities we observed at the No. 2 Middle School in Shanghai. Talented young people of all ages also attend after-school sessions at the children's palaces or neighborhood activity centers located in China's cities. We were also informed, but not shown, that many communes have centers where children can receive guidance in special areas during after-school hours. We actually visited only one such center: the model Shanghai Children's Palace is a standard feature of nearly every tour of Shanghai.

We were told that at least ten other centers existed in the city, but we were unable to make a comparison as to the quality of facilities of the other centers. Certainly the facilities and programs available at the children's palace we visited could not have been more ideal. We received no information on the availability of such facilities in China's rural areas.

It was our impression that extracurricular activities in China are designed to provide an extension of the same work that students do in their classrooms. While the youth we observed were obviously enjoying themselves, it was clear that they perceived themselves to be engaged in serious business which they could, and should, be able to relate directly to subjects of classroom study. One middle-school student made frequent references to mathematics and physics textbooks as he worked up a blueprint for the wing section of a model airplane he was building.

It was only after our hectic and very entertaining visit to the Shanghai Children's Palace that we were able to learn how students become eligible to use its facilities. Members of the staff of the No. 2 Shanghai Middle School related to us that only the brighter students are sent to the palace. They are given this added boost in the hope that they will benefit from working alongside other high achievers.

Community involvement is a mainstay in the operation of these after-school activity centers for bright students. The staff at the Shanghai Children's Palace, to cite one example, consists in the main of men and women who participate as activity leaders on a "voluntary" basis, in addition to their regular jobs. Only a few are full-time teachers by occupation; most work in factories, stores, and offices. We did not observe any members of the People's Liberation Army helping out at the children's palace. The director of the palace emphasized the varied nature of the backgrounds of the staff, repeating several times that this feature is regarded as a positive aspect of the environment of the palace.

A similar kind of community involvement occurs at a broader level and includes a significantly larger number of students. Schools at all levels have student organizations. In the primary schools, students wearing red neckerchiefs are members of the "Little Red Soldiers," while in the middle schools an armband proclaims that its bearer is a member of the more familiar "Red Guards." Finally, in the middle schools (usually upper middle schools) and in China's colleges and universities, some students become members of the Communist Youth League. The Little Red Soldiers were formerly known as the "Young Pioneers," but that organization was replaced in the aftermath of the Cultural Revolution. In the same way, the Red Guards emerged in their present form as a result of the Cultural Revolution and now seem to exist side-by-side with, but in a position somewhat inferior to, the Communist Youth League. All school classes in China come under the direction of a "Lead Teacher" of "Class Teacher." He or she is in turn assisted by "school cadres" who are always members of the Little Red Soldiers, the Red Guards, or the Communist Youth League. In a college or university this format changes but the Communist Youth League remains an active force in student life. Thus, a typical primary-school class would comprise some 45 to 50 students, two-thirds of whom would be members of the Little Red Soldiers and all of whom would identify one teacher as the "Class Teacher," even though they may be taught by as many as five or six teachers in all.

Activities designed to supplement the curriculum, apart from those sponsored by the children's palace and the neighborhood centers for children, are organized and conducted through the structure of one or more of the three political organizations for youth — the Little Red Soldiers, the Red Guards, and the Communist Youth League. Members of these organizations also take the lead in organizing their respective classes for yearly labor participation. As they conduct these activities they come into contact with members of the community who provide resources, advice, and leadership.

One illustration of this is the fact that exemplary workers often address meetings of the different student political organizations; so too do retired workers and workers with special skills. During periods of military training it is members of the Little Red Soldiers, the Red Guards, and the Communist Youth League who receive more individualized and intense instruction in drills and field problems. Of course, they are also expected to perform at a higher level and to carry a heavier burden than those who are not members of one of the organizations. Our point, however, is that community involvement is manifested in the area of political training both at the substantive level and also at a supplementary level. Community members such as exemplary workers or peasants and military representatives provide substantive information as part of regular political and moral education for all of the students. Yet they also provide leadership for those sectors of the student population who are more advanced in political terms as evidenced by their membership in student organizations. Thus certain sectors of the community that are highly prized for political-moral reasons become intimately associated with the emerging political elite among Chinese youth.

Another aspect of community involvement in local schools relates to the issue of local control and input into the formulation of education policy. While this has been discussed elsewhere in this report, we should note that our experience disabused us of certain conceptions we had had of the Chinese practice in this area. We had believed that schools were run by revolutionary committees whose membership included residents of the neighborhood. Indeed, all of the units we visited were administered by revolutionary committees, but in no case did the committee include local residents. When asked to describe the background of revolutionary committee members, our hosts responded with singular uniformity that the committee of a particular school was made up of teachers, "researchers," or other working staff of the school. Thus, nonprofessional representation on the revolutionary committees of schools we visited is confined to individuals who function as members of the professional staff and do not embrace "workers, peasants, and soldiers," even in the broadest sense of those terms. At the college and university level, revolutionary committees include students as well as staff, but here again in no case did we witness an instance of broadly based community participation in the process of directing the operation of local schools. When we confessed our surprise at this condition and cited press reports from 1971 to 1973 about the desirability of such participation, we occasioned some embarrassment on the part of our guides and hosts. The conversations we held subsequently with our guides indicated that there had been a movement at one time toward the concept of "neighborhood involvement" but that this (valid) concept had been "sabotaged" by the "Gang of Four" and therefore required "attention" and "research" before it could be reimplemented. It was, however, our opinion that such involvement runs counter to the present policy of standardization and professionalism and that the policy stands little chance of being widely or effectively practiced.

Thus our visit enabled us to discern that within certain limits parental and community involvement in the educational process is a desired goal, and further, that the goal is achieved in significant ways. In the areas we visited we ascertained that parental involvement is essentially supportive and is initiated and controlled essentially by the "professionals" in the schools. We also learned that Chinese parents have little ability to alter the classroom experiences of their children, that grandparents have an unusually large part of the responsibility for the social education of China's children, and that community involvement is significant in that it occurs across a wide range of areas — but that this too is supplementary to the school's definition of what is important at a particular time. In China, family and community involvement in formalized education is mobilized only when it is necessary to pursue standard education goals and to adjust to shifting policy preferences.

RELEVANCE TO AMERICAN NEEDS

Mary F. Berry

Assistant Secretary for Education,
U.S. Department of Health, Education and Welfare

As historians, several members of our delegation were especially sensitive to the fact that no social system exists apart from its historical context. Chinese education, like Chinese society itself, has been shaped and molded by the course of events since 1949 and before; what we witnessed in 1977 reflects policies and initiatives that had been adopted, transformed, or abandoned over the period of a generation. It is impossible for us to comprehend what we saw in China or to recognize its relevance (or lack of relevance) to America's educational needs without understanding the history of the recent past.

This discussion, therefore, will summarize that history and link it to what we learned of Chinese education in 1977. It will indicate those aspects of the system that are clearly abhorrent to most Americans, but will also suggest that there are fields in which educators in this nation stand to learn from their colleagues in China. The whole concept of comparative education is predicated on the assumption that different societies may benefit from one another's experiences. Those of us who went to China shared that assumption, and to varying degrees saw it reinforced during our time there.

It is important, however, to stress the limits of replicability. An effort to convert Western institutions into second-rate models of what exists elsewhere would be as impossible as it would be undesirable. Thousands of years of history and overwhelming differences in political ideology stand between our society and the Chinese. As Western imperialists learned a generation ago in China, it results in folly at best and tragedy at worst when one tries to superimpose one culture's ideology on another culture's people.

Americans and Chinese differ profoundly in several areas, as has been clear to even the most superficial analysts of our two systems. In the United States, intellectual freedom has historically been an ideal not always realized but aspired to nonetheless; the education system has been characterized by an avowed pursuit of an objectively defined, value-neutral "truth."

The Chinese we dealt with viewed truth in subjective terms, as at most a relative concept not identifiable except as part of a political construct. Its pursuit for its own sake they perceived as the worthless preoccupation of intellectual dilettantes; scholarly inquiry has value to them only insofar as it advances the political, economic, or technological interests of the society. In this context all educational pursuits, including basic research, have been infused with a revolutionary focus. As China scholar Peter Seybolt noted in the conclusion of his article "The Yenan Revolution in Mass Education," "the primary goal of education, according to Mao Tse-tung, is to change man's consciousness so as to change the world in which he lives." The path of change is not, in this view, to be determined by the individual alone; rather, it is to be the already predetermined Marxist path of liberation.

It was clear in 1977 that Mao's successors share this perspective. I was told quite explicitly by one of the officials of Peking University that in the contemporary view education must serve proletarian politics and should be combined with productive labor; everyone chosen to receive an education in China must develop what Chinese authorities call socialist consciousness and culture.

American analysts have often denounced that kind of approach. In so doing they have, however, ignored economic and historical factors that foster in the American system a greater level of tolerance. Educators in the United States have historically been acculturated to value freedom highly, because in a materially comfortable society they have been able to pursue it, by and large unfettered either by economic constraints or by the overwhelming and suffocating burden of a traditional caste system. Yet even in the United States there have been repeated calls to make the schools better serve the interests of the state: to turn out better, more literate workers and to guarantee that children become loyal and dutiful citizens. National rhetoric may proclaim the beauty of intellectual freedom, but short-run goals often belie that promise.

American education also differs from the Chinese in its emphasis on the individual student rather than on students as a class. Lawrence Cremin of the Columbia Teachers College expressed the conceptual question with which all American educational theorists working in this context have had to grapple: "A free society," he wrote, "concerns itself with individuals not masses. How, then, can the values of individuality be reconciled with the teaching of children in groups?" Attempts to answer this question have been at the heart of most innovations in American education, especially during the last decade. Open schools, free schools, schools without walls came (and, for the most part, went) as educators tried to find a mode of instruction that would respond to each student's individual needs. In various forms, that search has continued through the 1970s.

The Chinese are not distracted by such concerns with individuality. For them, education in its ideal form is a transfer of knowledge "from the masses to the masses" — in the words of a revolutionary slogan that dates back to the 1940s. It paints an overly grim picture of life in that society to say that they think of children as interchangeable parts. As do most cultures, the Chinese recognize the legitimacy of family relationships and have been willing to admit that some children learn at a slower pace than others. On the whole, however, they opt to view students as part of a mass, and deal with them as such.

An anecdote recounted by Uri Bronfenbrenner illustrates the point. On a visit to China, he asked his host:

"Yesterday at the commune we saw how the peasants were

conducting some experiments to see which kinds of soil and fertilizer were best for what kinds of plants. Why don't you do the same thing with children — study what kinds of environment are best for what kinds of youngsters?"
To which the Chinese educator replied patiently:
"You do not understand. All plants are different from each other, but it is important to believe that all children are the same."

However, my own observations did not confirm any supposition that Chinese education is completely regimented. I visited, during my curtailed stay of only six days in China, a nursery school, a day-care center, three primary schools (which in the United States would serve grades K-6), two middle schools, and several postsecondary facilities, and saw children who were better disciplined than their American counterparts, but far from automatons.

Political reporting offered a more accurate predicter of what we would see in China than did educational commentary. The image of China that Americans have received from the media has followed these basic lines: Over the past several years, Mao Tse-tung grew steadily weaker, both physically and mentally. Still revered by the public and regarded by the world as the great revolutionary leader of our time, Mao nonetheless had by 1975 become little more than a figurehead in whose name competing factions warred for power. Beneath the surface (and sometimes at the surface) there existed profound conflicts between the revolutionists, led by Mao's wife Chiang Ch'ing, and the technocrats, who had no clear leader but seemed to look to Teng Hsiao-p'ing as their symbolic champion. Teng had been disgraced in the Cultural Revolution when Chiang Ch'ing and her left-wing colleagues were at the peak of their power. On the death of Chou En-lai in early 1976, Teng was briefly rehabilitated, then disgraced again, and finally made a glorious comeback shortly before Mao's death. With Teng's political revival came the downfall of Chiang Ch'ing and her cohorts, by 1977 denounced in the Chinese press and abroad as the notorious "Gang of Four."

To the ordinary layman, or even to the apolitical educator, all of this was perplexing. Yet it has great significance here, for the ideology battles in education, as in every other sector of Chinese society, have been fought against the backdrop of these power plays. To the American mind, recent Chinese history has seemed very nearly incomprehensible; attempts to draw analogies to our own system have made it seem ludicrous. It is difficult to imagine, for example, Rosalynn Carter in league with the Secretary of Defense, the Secretary of Labor, and Hamilton Jordan working to seize power — and running up against the Chairman of the National Commission on Productivity and the Secretary of State. To take the analogy a step further, one should try to imagine that much of the conflict centered at least rhetorically on the correct interpretation of Jimmy Carter's book, Why Not the Best?

In any event, by the time of Mao's death, the technocrats were in the ascendancy and the Gang of Four were in disgrace. Of course, the "Gang" consisted of more than four people; Chiang Ch'ing and her associates had left-wing followers throughout the society. As has sometimes been the case in the United States, a vital segment of the basic left-wing constituency was comprised of youth; the Red Guards may have passed into history but their legacy remained strong.

It is not surprising, therefore, that education became a primary arena in which the great power struggle would be waged. Events did not move in an orderly fashion, but the basic image America received was as follows: In its season in power, the left wing seized control of the academic establishment; it enforced a massive dislocation of faculty and students and attempted to weed out all vestiges of traditional Confucianist thought. In the process, careers were destroyed, lives lost, academic standards lowered to the vanishing point, and the Chinese intellectual community all but obliterated. Robert Scalapino outlined their view in his article, "The Struggle Over Higher Education — Revolution Versus Development": "The resulting dominance of politics over professionalism has resulted in turning out students who are hopelessly incompetent, reducing graduate studies and theoretical research to a bare minimum and lowering the morale of all intellectuals to a dangerous level."

Intellectualism, in this view, was all but dead in the waning days of Mao's life. Fearful of the development and perpetuation of an educated elite, and even more fearful of development of a higher education system "more Soviet than Chinese," Mao strove to make each education institution a locus for role-switching among intellectuals and workers and, through this process, status equalization. The "July 21" colleges where workers were admitted to study to become engineers constituted part of this effort at social transformation. The half-work, half-study system which required students to spend half their time working among the people was a more integral element, one that met with resistance upon its adoption in 1958 but came into full effect in the mid-1960s. More central still to Mao's campaign to root elitism out of education was his effort to open admissions to postsecondary schools to all people, giving preferential help to those from worker backgrounds. Once he got such people into school, Mao wanted to make sure they stayed in over the resistance of faculty holdovers with more traditional ideas.

It has been difficult for Americans to understand the extreme rigidity of the Chinese class system and the surprising extent to which that rigidity lasted in education well into the Maoist era. Partly it had its roots in the fact that opportunities for higher education have historically been sharply limited in China. Even in 1977 there were only 400,000 people enrolled in the universities in a nation whose population was fast approaching 900 million; there were in the same year about 400,000 college students in the state of Ohio. Progress was being made in extending education at other levels; middle-school enrollments went from 1.4 million to about 40 million in 1977. With university admissions so limited, however, it was to be expected that this would lead to status differentiation and that acceptance should be so highly prized. Prior to the post-World War II years, the situation was much the same in the United States.

The examination system, both for admissions and graduation, came to be seen as the primary barrier keeping working-class Chinese out of the university. Just as tests in the United States, from IQ tests in the early years to college boards later on, served as cultural roadblocks to minorities and the poor, so the admissions examinations in China served the same purpose.

Mao did not move to eliminate tests until the late 1960s, but he did try to subvert them. He went so far as to advise in 1964 that

> in examinations, students should be allowed to whisper to each other and to hire others to take the examinations for them.... Copying is good, too.... Examinations are designed for dealing with the enemy. They poison people to death and should be abolished.

It would be interesting to see the public and academic reaction to a statement of that kind by an American president. In China, the reaction came soon: Examinations were, by and large, done away with and by the 1970s political dedication had become the primary (and in some cases the only) criterion of admission to the university. Mao had once called for a student body both red and expert. By the early part of the decade it was only necessary that one be sufficiently red.

As can be imagined, the overthrow of the tyrannical examination system immediately became a popular cause with Chinese students. The Gang of Four exploited this; they made a national hero out of a student who turned in a blank test paper, and denounced the imposition of any kind of discipline. It was the U.S. system of the late 1960s writ large.

There was an almost inevitable reaction to the excesses that resulted, and by 1977 we saw a limited reinstatement of some aspects of the traditional education system. To contend that the Gang of Four's overthrow precipitated a counterrevolution in education is, however, an overstatement. Many of the Maoist reforms imposed in the 1960s were intact in 1977.

The Chinese had not, for example, terminated their policy of bringing workers into the university or of putting students to work; nor had they restored the examination to its previously exalted status or eliminated political considerations as criteria of admissions. They had modified policy in a few of these areas and are thinking about modifying it in others, but the thrust of the Maoist reforms — the effort to broaden access, to make schooling responsive to the state and the people — remained still a dominant theme.

News accounts in the United States had indicated that under the pragmatists the Chinese abandoned their policy (once a cornerstone of Mao's program) of having students return to the countryside after what we would call high school. Instead, reports contended, chosen students were going to go directly to the university, as is the usual pattern in the United States. This, so far as personal observation could indicate, was a gross overstatement. In fact, no changes had taken place by late 1977. A new enrollment policy had been announced in general terms, but discussions were still in progress on its implementation, and as a result there was no new class in school in the fall semester of that year. Since our visit, however, the use of tests has been instituted and a new class has been selected.

The tentative projections the Chinese made were that only 20 to 30 percent of the university students would come straight from secondary school, and almost all of those would be enrolled in specific fields (primarily the sciences) where the Chinese believe a sequential education is almost essential. Chinese officials asserted that all students in middle schools as well as in elementary schools would still be spending part of their time as workers or peasants. Even for the favored few the Chinese did not project a complete reversion to the straight academic track system.

The Chinese leaders indicated that they were only willing to go this far because they saw the need for a strong cadre of research scientists if the modernization efforts were to make progress through the rest of the century. The phrase they used to describe their goal was an illustrative one: China, they said, has to be able to "walk on two legs" — to be self-reliant and draw on both communist ideology and technical expertise.

This represented no abandonment of the revolution. Nor did the fact that on a limited basis the Chinese reimposed admissions examinations. In order to accelerate modernization, the leaders began to express renewed support for tests in 1977 and contended that Mao always had as well; yet it was clear that the test results would represent only one of the bases on which enrollment decisions will be made. "Bad" class background would still be an eliminating factor, as would ideology. Peer recommendations remained as important as they were at the peak of the Cultural Revolution. The Chinese indicated that they would continue to impose admissions quotas, as they had since 1972, for people from each geographic region and each minority ethnic group.

It was interesting to me, and I think should be of concern to most Americans in education, that in this last respect the Chinese were moving rationally and realistically in a field that led to confusion and near-hysteria in the United States. Of course, the nondemocratic nature of Chinese society facilitated the imposition of a centrally monitored admissions system and undoubtedly served to forestall criticism from those excluded from postsecondary education through the quota program. Beyond this, however, there were more positive aspects to the Chinese support for the system; it reflected acceptance of the need for special programs to reach disadvantaged groups and support for the concept of opportunity equalization.

The Chinese have not, moreover, abandoned their disdain for what they consider aimless intellectualism. One recent propaganda publication told of the horrors of education under domination of the Gang of Four, and concluded (ironically) with the following illustration:

> The worst result was the students' concern for themselves rather than for serving the people. When one biology graduate did not realize his hopes of becoming a teaching assistant or a researcher, he took a job that had nothing to do with what he had spent years studying just so he could stay in the city and not go to the countryside where he had been assigned. Of what use were university graduates like this to a China building socialism?

Similar questions have, of course, been raised in the United

States, particularly by legislators grappling with education appropriation requests. Chinese concern that education be well utilized has been heightened by the enormous investment in each university student; while budget figures are unavailable, it is clear that their teacher-student ratio is extremely low — about six to one, compared with eleven to one at a typical American school. The stakes are much higher for the Chinese, therefore, in guaranteeing that the recipients of an education put it to use for the good of society.

The whole relationship between the academy and the real world represents an area in which American society may have much to learn from the Chinese. There are, as indicated earlier, cultural distinctions which make a complete emulation impractical. Americans would, however, do well to look at what the Chinese have been doing to unify education with the world of work and adapt it to this society's needs.

About seven years ago the United States, under the last Administration, embarked on a program called "Career Education," which was supposed to represent a major new development in national education policy. A great many people have had some trouble with the way that effort has been administered. The concepts behind it were valid ones, though, and the problems it was supposed to address were real. By most objective appraisals, there has been too much age segregation in American society, too little sense of purpose among our youth, too little familiarity with the norms and disciplines of the workplace; there are, moreover, too many unemployed BA's, and too many people in college who are there because they lack a clear sense of purpose. The problems do not yet represent national crises, but they will if the society fails to address them in a positive way.

Career education was supposed to be the American vehicle for dealing with each of these difficulties. The program orientation was simple: From the earliest grades, administrators were to infuse curricula with work-oriented instruction. Workers at every level (technicians, professionals, factory workers, and others) were to be invited into the schools to explain to children the kind of work they do and what training they need to do it. Older children would be placed in the community working for credit on a part-time basis at a variety of jobs as they formulate their career goals. Through such a program, educators would assure that the only people going to college went because they believed that the education they were to receive there had some relevance to their lives and aspirations.

Career education has not yet worked here. There are a great many economic, bureaucratic, and philosophical reasons for that. It is clear that American society still has a long way to go before it can accept John Dewey's basic idea (which the Chinese accepted long ago) that "education (should be) life, not preparation for life."

In China, we witnessed in some places a nearly complete unity between education and labor — so complete that both activities came to seem a basic, natural part of life, as they should be. We saw for example elementary school children six years old spending an hour out of every day working at producing voice boxes for dolls which were to be sold to a factory, with the proceeds paying part of the school's operating costs, and other young children in crafts classes producing other items on consignment. At the middle school level, we saw schools associated with factories producing automobile parts; at the next level, technical schools (which are analogous to the last two years of our high schools) were working directly with industry. At universities, science students worked directly in laboratories. Other examples could be cited, but the point is clear: The Chinese were trying to bridge the gap between the world of the scholar and the world of the worker by merging the two worlds into one.

Obviously we have no desire to put six-year-olds to work here; adult unemployment has been a serious enough problem without the displacement by children of adults from productive jobs. Many Americans do see a need to work more aggressively to implement a realistic education and work strategy — one that in the context of American culture and a capitalist economy addresses the basic problem of alienation of workers from labor. The Chinese have offered this society a useful model in that effort.

The Chinese experience is useful in the broader area of development of a workable program in education for adults that meets needs for intellectual fulfillment and social growth. It is here that our observations led us to believe that the Chinese set a pattern for the world to follow; it is, coincidentally, here that American higher education may have one of its best opportunities for growth. In the context of declining enrollment and declining public willingness to support traditional postsecondary education, most American institutions are compelled to reach out beyond their traditional constituency and attract and enroll workers, retired people, and others who heretofore have been excluded by life circumstance and by tradition.

This practice has been basic to Chinese education since the success of the revolution in 1949. It has survived periods of revision and periods of revolutionary change since then, and it continues in full flower today. Every class in the Chinese university system is a mixture of people from all backgrounds — peasants and factory workers, urban and rural people, and people of different ages. While most students are under thirty, the student bodies otherwise represent a heterogeneous ideal. Although the Chinese do not point explicitly to this as an advantage, it is clear that the students can learn from one another as well as from their instructors. People from varied backgrounds, primarily from outside the academic community, participate in the governance of the institutions as well.

American society is moving slowly toward a similar situation. The community college system, with its nonconventional enrollment, is one harbinger for change; the traditional extension program is another. Those efforts have had positive results and indicate that it will be feasible to go further and bring four-year institutions and secondary institutions, as well as private instructional facilities, into the lifelong learning movement.

This seems clearly to represent the course of the future of

American education. The society has started to lift most of the other barriers to participation. While the United States still has a long way to go before equal opportunity regardless of race or sex is a reality, it is moving toward a system of universal inclusivity. The next major step would logically appear to be opening the benefits of education to all people, regardless of age or intent to pursue a formal degree program. In taking that step, American educators may well wish to look to the Chinese experience for whatever guidance it can provide. Again, it must be emphasized that in studying the Chinese effort in this particular area, Americans need accept neither the philosophical premises nor the economic assumptions that underlie Chinese society in general. The Chinese effort to include the previously excluded is simply one aspect of a comprehensive education system worthy of analysis and, with modification to conform to the needs of our own culture, limited emulation.

A sense of realism and fairmindedness should bring all Americans to the conviction that their ultimate goals in education may well be shared by people and societies whose ideologies differ from our own. It is for this reason that it is important for American educators to understand what it is the Chinese have been doing to relate education to work, to involve the previously excluded in all education programs, and to improve their system in other ways. Our delegation's exposure to China's education system did nothing to shake our faith in the validity of basic American precepts concerning intellectual freedom. It did, however, convince us that in a few critical areas, American teachers and education administrators stand to learn much from their Chinese counterparts. The Chinese have much to learn from us if they are to succeed in modernizing their society.

CONCLUSIONS

Ralph W. Tyler

Director, Chicago Program of the Center
for the Study of Democratic Institutions

Each of the foregoing chapters is a report of the observations made by individual members of the delegation and their interpretations of what they saw and heard. The statements made in this chapter represent the tentative conclusions we have drawn based on the points emphasized in the other chapters and on our own impressions of education in China. We hope they will stimulate further observations and reports from future delegations as well as provoking discussion now.

The first and foremost conclusion which is supported by the observations of all members of our delegation is the importance attached to education. It is quite clear that the Party leaders set a very high priority on developing an effective educational system. They depend upon education as the chief means for achieving the goals of the continuing revolution, which include an economic system providing the material basis for a prosperous nation and a healthy, happy people; a classless society in which all citizens are striving to "serve the people"; and a powerful, modern nation secure in its defenses and a leader in world affairs. Every modern nation including the United States places heavy dependence on education as a means for achieving its goals. Our economy is based on a high level of technology that requires educated persons to design, operate and use appropriately these systems of production and distribution. Our democratic political system requires educated citizens to guide and control our states and nation without destruction. Our commitment to equality and appreciation of diversity require education to free our people from prejudice and narrow self-interest. Our opportunities for social mobility have been implemented by educational opportunity rather than by a massive redistribution of wealth. The demands on our educational system are severe.

In one aspect the Chinese expect even more than we. Their commitment to a classless society in which all citizens "serve the people" requires the inculcation of new values that are at the very heart of personal and social development. In the traditional family most children throughout the world are reared in an environment that emphasizes self-preservation and responsibility for other family members. As a result children grow up with a strong sense of self-interest and responsibility for members of their group, especially their family, but without a compelling urge to serve people who are not identified with the family. To shift this priority of personal values, attitudes, and habits is a difficult educational task, yet it is central to communist ideology.

The most difficult task for a mass democratic nation is to help the individual achieve fully his own ideal of uniqueness. However, democratic societies are committed to respect for each individual, to appreciation of the diversity of human characteristics and achievements, and to the encouragement of self-realization. The American educational system makes significant contributions to this purpose but its full attainment is not yet realized.

A second conclusion drawn from our observations and the statements made by our hosts is that Chinese educational policy, like that of the United States, is not always moving in one direction but includes reversals from time to time. These shifts in policy have been described and explained by Ronald Montaperto. They are due in some cases to shifting emphasis on national objectives and in others to the unanticipated consequences of certain policies. The Cultural Revolution was a response to the growing elitism of university-educated persons, which was seriously impeding progress toward the goal of a classless society. The criteria for admission to the universities were changed to emphasize proletarian background, excellent work record, and devotion to the continuing revolution.

But this new basis for admission produced some unanticipated consequences. The university students admitted according to these criteria were largely activists. Few of them were interested in abstract ideas and theories. They were not putting forth the effort to become scientists, mathematicians, linguists, or philosophers. The universities were not producing the intellectual leaders required to make China a leading industrial nation and world power by the year 2000. Yet this was one of the chief goals of the Party. After bitter debate the Central Committee voted to discontinue the admission policy formulated as part of the Cultural Revolution and to place intellectual interests and abilities as a primary criterion for admission. This policy was quickly approved by the Party Congress.

This reversal of educational policy was apparently due to two factors. The former policy produced unanticipated consequences. Furthermore, the former policy was intended to achieve the goal of a classless society, but the later debate resulted in a decision that placed priority on the goal of becoming a strong national state by the year 2000. Educational policies in the United States have shifted from time to time for one or both of these reasons.

A third conclusion is that China places high priority on political education. This term seems to mean training children, youth, and adults to appreciate the contributions made by the Communist Party to the development of the nation, to understand and accept the role of the communist citizen, and to value and practice communist morality. Abraham Lincoln characterized our political system as "of the people, by the people and for the people." The Chinese political system could be described as "for the people." The responsibility for planning and directing the nation is held by the Communist Party. The role of the citizen is to respect and follow the leadership of the Party. The communist principles of morality furnish the rationale for this control.

The four basic principles of morality as formulated by the Party are: (1) love of country; (2) devotion to serving the people; (3) guiding one's actions by the decisions of one's group; and (4) respect for constituted authority. Three of these principles are consistent with the moral codes of the Western world. McGuffey's readers, for example, included many stories glorifying love of America, serving others, and respect for law, parents, teachers, and other constituted authorities. But the moral tradition of the Western world posits abstract principles of right and wrong. McGuffey included a number of stories in which the hero stood up against his peers. The hero had a conscience that helped him decide the right thing to do. The peer group decision was not the highest authority in determining the right.

Maoism, like the Marxism-Leninism of the Soviet Union, defines immorality as deviation from the group. We were not told how this view developed. Perhaps it came from the philosophy of dialectical materialism or perhaps from the necessity to justify the communist leadership practice in which the revolutionary committee in the organization states the action to be followed and imposes sanctions on those who deviate. But the instructional emphasis from the kindergarten through the primary and middle schools is based upon these four principles of morality. Through didactic instruction, through the organization of activities in the schools, through work experiences and the activities in the children's palaces and youth palaces, the values, attitudes, practices, and rationale of the Chinese political system are continually reiterated and reinforced. This heavy emphasis upon political education attracted our interest particularly because citizenship education in the United States has not received in this century the attention required to develop a comprehensive, constructive program.

A fourth conclusion is that China is making a strong effort to integrate education for work and for citizenship. Maoism gives heavy emphasis to the work ethic. The economic salvation of the communist regime was the speed with which the millions of unemployed and underemployed Chinese were put to work in producing food and other necessities for subsistence. The earlier chapter on education for work describes the great emphasis given to work in Chinese schools and colleges.

Prior to the Revolution, China was highly stratified into several social classes. The ruling class did not participate in work with the hands, and the proletariat did not participate in the political affairs of the nation. Education was aimed to prepare the ruling classes with the knowledge, skills, and attitudes appropriate for their responsibilities, and what little formal training was given the proletariat was to enable them to do their work properly and skillfully. Political education was for rulers, training for work was for the proletariat. The educational plan of the communist regime is intended to teach all Chinese people to work, to understand politics from the perspective of Marxism, and to appreciate the political leadership provided by the Communist Party. Hence, the educational plan calls for the integration into a single curriculum education for work and for citizenship.

The Western nations also went through a period of sharp social and political stratification, and the formal educational systems of the West also originated during a period when the ruling classes were provided with liberal education and the working classes with training for the jobs they were to perform. In America, as in other Western nations, we are still struggling to try to integrate occupational and general education. We have found it to be a difficult task but one necessary if we are to attain our democratic aspirations as a nation in which all persons contribute to the society through their work and participate in the affairs of the state with understanding of the issues and guided by a deep concern for the general welfare. We were not able to judge in our brief visit how effective Chinese education has been in integrating work and politics, but the intensity of their effort was obvious.

A fifth conclusion we drew was that the Chinese leaders recognize the great importance of the non-school learning environment. The children's palaces, the youth palaces, the harvest brigades, the work experiences outside the school are all part of the educational system for which objectives appear to be formulated and some form of supervision furnished. We saw no young person alone without some form of supervision or guidance.

This planning for the constructive use of out-of-school learning opportunities is in contrast to the situation in most parts of the United States. In America, out-of-school learning activities like those provided by the children's palaces and the youth palaces are available to some children and youth, but we have no system to assure that all children make constructive use of their out-of-school time. In an earlier period most parents were clear about their responsibilities. Many children had chores at home and part-time jobs and young people could participate in community activities. Now those learning activities have been greatly reduced. This is a serious problem. The Chinese experience should stimulate us to rebuild the total learning environment of our young people. Otherwise the great educational demands of our modern society cannot be met.

A sixth conclusion is that China has not yet developed a firm decision regarding the degree of centralization or decentralization in the control of education that should be established. The earlier chapters described the different degrees of decentralization that have existed in the brief periods into which the Chinese communist experience can be divided. The shifts in policy regarding centralized financial support of schools and universities, decentralized curriculum development, centralized selection of university students, decentralized supervision and control of the instructional staff have been mentioned. Not only have there been changes in these policies from time to time, but in each period examples of mixed policies were described. Apparently China, like the Western nations, finds it difficult to formulate educational policy regarding decentralization. This is probably due to two factors: conflicting goals to be achieved and the difficulty, if not impossibility, of controlling professional functions at a distance from those who carry on these functions.

The purposes of centralization in China appear to be: (1) to use resources in ways that maximize their contributions in meeting the needs of the state; (2) to facilitate comprehensive planning and decision making for all sectors of the nation; and (3) to ensure continued control by the Communist Party, particularly its Central Committee. These purposes might indicate the desirability of centralization of all aspects of education. However, Mao learned from the experience of the Soviet Union that regions some distance from the central authority do not willingly reveal all their assets for fear they will be taken away. Hence, some degree of decentralization is likely to encourage localities to use their assets to support activities they desire.

This would seem to account for the decentralization of some part of the support of schools, especially during the period when the central government lacked the funds required to support all of the desired educational activities. Another generalization about centralization is that persons affected by public policies who have had no part in formulating and approving them are likely to take little responsibility for the actions the policies require. On the other hand, for example, if it is my school, for my children to learn things I want them to have a chance to learn, so I am likely to do what I can to help the school carry on its work effectively.

Whereas centralization is an important principle of communist ideology, to be modified only when necessary, the political theory generally espoused in the United States is that the function of the state is to facilitate the development of the individual, that the state should not legislate conformity but rather should encourage diversity, and that the control of the state should be the responsibility of all citizens, exercised through their freely elected representatives. In accordance with these principles, centralization in education has been approved only to ensure a wide basis of financial support and when necessary for the national defense or the general welfare. Hence, the American tradition has been one of a highly decentralized educational system, involving centralization only at times or in aspects that can be justified as necessary for adequate support, or for the national defense or the general welfare.

The direction or guidance of professional functions poses a special problem for centralized governments. The financing of education, the building of schools, the selection and assignment of teachers, and the admission of students can be directed from a central authority, but the process of education goes on in classrooms and other sites where teachers and students are interacting. If the teacher does not believe in the educational objective, if he does not understand his role in attaining it, if he does not have the skill required for his role, or lacks confidence that he can carry it out, the desired learning is not likely to happen no matter how forcefully it is decreed. Centralized control of professional functions like education is very different from the control of highway construction. China, like the United States, has not yet developed a doctrine to guide policies in this area. The problem of the Chinese Central Committee is how to decentralize education sufficiently to encourage local effort and initiative, to gain wholehearted cooperation of the local teaching staffs without losing control.

A seventh conclusion we drew was that the Chinese have not yet developed a comprehensive theory of learning and teaching that is adequate for the educational goals that have been established. Within the classrooms we saw a great deal of rote learning. It appeared to be conditioning. The term conditioning is commonly used to refer to the behavior that is initiated by a clear stimulus and consists of an automatic fixed response.

We saw a great deal of what could be called conditioning in the classrooms we visited. The method of group instruction begins with the teacher asking a question, then calling on a student for the answer. The student chosen to respond is one who has usually given correct answers, so the teacher rarely has to turn to a second student because the one called on first did

not give a correct response. When the correct response is
given the teacher repeats it and then calls on the class to repeat
the correct answer. The class intones this response several
times with enthusiasm as the teacher smiles, applauds, and
joins in the repetitive chanting of the answer. No doubt, this
method of rote learning inculcates the right answers in the
minds of most children. It reinforces the group response
to group leaders who represent constituted authorities.

Conditioning can be effective in developing conformity, fixed
habits, and static beliefs and attitudes. But as China seeks to
become a modern industrial nation it must develop persons who
question present answers to complex problems, whose curiosity
seeks satisfaction through new inquiries, and who will be formulating new theories, solving new problems, and developing new
systems to apply constructively the new knowledge. Rote
learning is not an adequate basis for developing modern scientists, engineers, and philosophers. Some of the Chinese educational leaders appear to recognize the need for developing a
theory of learning and teaching that includes conditioning but
also furnishes the basis for the teaching of problem finding,
problem solving, and creative invention. The fact that when we
asked to look at instructional materials in the middle schools
and sought to discuss learning theory, we were told that they
were working on these matters and had nothing yet to show, indicated that the Chinese leaders recognize the incompleteness
of or inadequacy of their theory. We also believe that there is
work going on to try to construct a comprehensive concept to
guide teaching and learning at the middle-school level.

Finally, we should like to comment, as have other visitors to
China, on the warm but hierarchical relations between students
and teachers. It seemed clear that almost all children liked
their teachers and felt warmly toward them. It also appeared
to us that teachers had similar feelings toward their students.
But it was not the affection of peers. The teachers seemed to
have internalized the slogan "serve the people" and sincerely
appreciated the responsibility they had to help children become

socially constructive adults. Similarly, the children seemed to understand that the teachers cared about them and wanted to help them. The children respected teachers as higher authorities. Their respect was not born of fear, but of appreciation for devoted service.

We hope that this report from the members of our delegation makes clear that our trip to study briefly the educational system of the People's Republic of China was not only an interesting one but highly instructive as well. We learned from observing education in a very different culture and context a number of things that helped us to understand more fully the progress and problems of education in the United States, and gained as well some insights into the efforts of a large and populous nation to shape an educational system to serve its political, economic, and social goals.

APPENDICES

Itinerary

Friday, October 28, Peking

    Morning   Arrival at Peking Airport

                HU Shou-hsin, Responsible Person, External Affairs Bureau, Ministry of Education, Peking
                CHANG, Yin-hsien, Department of Higher Education, Ministry of Education
                HU Hsu-chih, External Affairs Bureau, Ministry of Education*
                CHI Hsiao-lin, Interpreter, External Affairs Bureau, Ministry of Education*
                CHAO Ying-nan (f) Interpreter, Office of Peking Foreign Language Institute*

    Afternoon   No. 1 Peking Experimental Primary School

                CHANG Shan, Revolutionary Committee Chairman
                CHU Chieh-chih, Vice Chairman
                LI Chih-kuang (f), Vice Chairman
                TENG Chih-mou (f), Vice Chairman

---

*Escorted delegation throughout China.

Evening   Welcoming Banquet, Great Hall of the People
   LI Ch'i, Vice Minister of Education, host
   CHOU P'ei-yuan, Vice Chairman of the Chinese People's Institute of Foreign Affairs and Vice Chairman of the Revolutionary Committee of Peking University
   KANG Tai-hsia, Deputy Secretary General of the Chinese People's Institute of Foreign Affairs
   SU Lin, Chairman of the Revolutionary Committee of Peking Languages Institute
   HAN Tso-lin, Responsible Person, Education Bureau of Peking
   LIEN Cheng-pao, Deputy Chief, American Affairs Division, Department of American and Oceanian Affairs, Ministry of Foreign Affairs
   LIN Chen-chun, Professor of Physics, Peking Normal University

   HU Shou-hsin   CHI Hsiao-lin
   HU Hsu-chih   CHAO Ying-nan

Saturday, October 29, Peking

Morning   Visit to Mao Tse-tung Mausoleum
   No. 2 Peking Kindergarten of Ch'ung-wen District
   HSIEH Chi-mei (f), Vice Chairman of School Revolutionary Committee
   CH'ANG Kuang-jung (f), Vice Chairman of School Revolutionary Committee

Afternoon   Visit to the Forbidden City
Evening   Music Concert

Sunday, October 30, Peking

Morning/   Visit to the Great Wall and the Ming
Afternoon   Tombs

Itinerary 177

Evening   Meeting with Minister of Education LIU Hsi-yao at the International Club

         HU Shou-hsin
         Delegation escorts (4)
         Mr. David Dean, Deputy Chief, U.S. Liaison Office, Peking
         Mr. Charles Sylvester, U.S. Liaison Office

Monday, October 31, Peking

Morning   Visit to Peking University

         CHOU P'ei-yuan, Vice Chairman, Revolutionary Committee, Peking University
         NI Meng-hsiung, Leading Member, Office of the Revolutionary Committee, PU; Lecturer of Russian
         CHANG Chih-lien, Professor of History
         YEN Chih-chieh, Professor of Economics
         YU Hsin-pao, Cadre, PU Revolutionary Committee
         YEH T'ing-hsing, Student Representative, PU Revolutionary Committee and student of Western Languages

Afternoon   Visit to Peking Normal University

         WANG Hsiang, Responsible Person, PNU Revolutionary Committee
         KU Ming-yuan (f), Instructor of Childhood Revolutionary Education
         CHEN Chung-wen, Office worker, PNU Revolutionary Committee
         LIN Chen-chin, Professor of Physics
         CHEN Hsiao-ping, Professor, Education Department
         CHANG Chih-kuang, Professor, Education Department
         LIN Ping, Professor, Education Department

178　China's Schools in Flux

                LI Shuang-li, Cadre, Revolutionary Committee of PNU

Evening   Delegation Return Banquet in honor of the Ministry of Education, Chin Yang Restaurant

                LI Ch'i, Vice Minister of Education, principal guest
                KANG Tai-hsia (f)
                SU Lin
                HAN Tso-lin
                LIEN Cheng-pao
                LIN Chen-chun
                HU Shou-hsin
                NI Meng-hsiung
                WANG Hsiang
                Delegation escorts (3)
                Drivers (8)

Tuesday, November 1, Peking

Morning   Visit to Peking Opera School

                MA Hsiu-fang (f), Ministry of Culture Official
                YEN Hsiu-hsun, Ministry of Culture Official
                LI Chiao, Chairman, Peking Opera School Revolutionary Committee
                KAO Shen-ling, Vice Chairman, POS Revolutionary Committee
                LI Hua-yun (f), Chief of Opera Section, POS

Afternoon Discussion at hotel with over 150 Chinese colleagues who work in administration and policy formulation at the Ministry of Education, the Peking Education Bureau and several of the "Key" schools in the Peking area. Discussion group one focused on elementary and secondary education; discussion group two centered on higher education in the United States.

Evening   Reception at the United States Liaison Office hosted by Mr. David Dean, Deputy Chief, and his wife.

Travel to Nanking on an overnight train

Wednesday, November 2, Nanking

Morning   Arrival and briefing on Nanking Schedule

FANG Fei (f), Deputy Chief, Kiangsu Province Bureau of Education
YI Hou-chen, Deputy Leader, Kiangsu Province Office of Higher Education
CHOU Sung-san, Nanking University Foreign Affairs Office Chief
CH'ANG Ning-sa, Nanking Normal College Revolutionary Committee Office Head
FANG Wei-ming, Kiangsu Province Foreign Affairs Office worker
YEN   , Kiangsu Province Foreign Affairs Office worker
HSIEH Chia-p'i, Kiangsu Province Education Bureau worker

Afternoon   Visit to Purple Mountain Astronomical Observatory

Visit to Nanking Power School

TAN Yu-lin, Vice Chairman, NPS Revolutionary Committee (speaker)
WU Pei-yin, NPS Teacher
CHIN He-ken, NPS Teacher
CHOU Ying-wen, NPS Teacher
LI Fu-ting, Chairman, NPS Revolutionary Committee

Evening   Banquet in honor of the delegation at the Nanking Hotel, Madame Fang Fei, host

Discussion with Madame Fang immediately following banquet; Madame Fang spoke on the current education situation in Kiangsu Province.

Thursday, November 3, Nanking and Yangchou

Morning Visit to Nanking Normal College

  CHANG Wan-t'ing, Vice Chairman, NNC Revolutionary Committee
  TSAO Ch'i-p'ing, Dean of the Language Department
  HUI Hung (f), Dean of the Biology Department
  SUN Jui-ching, Head of the Teaching Group, NNC Foreign Language Department
  YEH Hsu-teh, NNC Revolutionary Committee Secretary, Professor of Education

Afternoon Visit to Nanking Bridge

  Drive to Yangchou

Evening Arrival in Yangchou, welcoming remarks and a welcoming banquet in honor of the delegation at the hotel, NING Yu-tsang, principal host.

  NING Yu-tsang, Chief of Yangchou Prefecture Bureau of Education
  WANG Shou-chuan, Yangchou Prefecture External Affairs Office Worker
  SUN Po-ching (f), Yangchou Prefecture Education Office worker
  YAN Wei-ting, Yangchou Prefecture External Affairs Office Worker

Friday, November 4, Yangchou

Morning Visit to Huai River Flood Control Project

Afternoon Visits to Lacquerware, Jade and Paper Cutting Factories in Yangchou

Evening   Drive to Nanking and board late train to Hangchou

Saturday, November 5, Hangchou

    Morning   Arrival in Hangchou

    Afternoon   Visit to Running Tiger Spring

    Evening   Free

Sunday, November 6, Hangchou

    Morning   Boat Trip on West Lake

    Afternoon   Visit to Hangchou Silk Factory

    Evening   Discussion in hotel with Mr. Hu, our escort from Peking. Topic was the Ministry of Education.

Monday, November 7, Hangchou

    Morning   Visit to An-chi-lu Primary School

                   SUNG Ping (f), Chairman, School Revolutionary Committee
                   CH'ING Ken-ying (f), Teacher
                   TUNG Yueh-chu (f), Teacher

    Afternoon   Visit to Mei-chia-wu Production Brigade

                   CHEN Wu-yun (f), Vice Chairman, Brigade Revolutionary Committee (preschool)

    Evening   Train to Shanghai

                   Arrival and Welcome at Hotel Chinchiang

                   CH'EN Yuan, No. 1 Vice Chairman, Shanghai Education Bureau
                   CH'EN Ch'i, No. 3 Vice Chairman, Shanghai Education Bureau
                   LI Li (f), Director of Spare-time Education for Workers and Peasants, Shanghai Bureau

YU Li, Director of Primary and Middle Schools, Shanghai Education Bureau
WANG Teh-ming, Interpreter, Teacher of English, Futan University
FU Wei-chung, Shanghai Education Bureau worker, Principal organizer of our stay in Shanghai
LU Kuo-ch'ang, Futan University English Department Director of Education
TU Hsu-chuan, Shanghai Education Bureau External Affairs Official
NIEN   , Working Staff, Shanghai Education Bureau

Tuesday, November 8, Shanghai

Morning   Visit to Tsao-yang Workers Residential Quarters (preschool)

CHU Feng-yun (f), Leading Comrade, Neighborhood Revolutionary Committee
SHIH Wen-yueh (f), Responsible Person, Neighborhood Kindergarten
HUANG Ming (f), Staff Member, Residential Quarters
KANG Mou-ying (f), Kindergarten Staff Member

Afternoon Visit to No. 2 Lower and Upper Middle School of Shanghai

LU Fu (f), School Principal
KUEI Shou-kang, Vice Principal

Evening   No program except shopping at Friendship Store

Wednesday, November 9, Shanghai

Morning   Visit to Hua-shan Hospital

WANG Te-chao, Chief Surgeon

LIN Shun-yun, Director of Internal Medicine
LU Chun (f), Internal Medicine Office Director

Afternoon Visits to First Department Store of Shanghai, Book Store of Foreign Languages, and the Shanghai Children's Palace

Evening Performance of the Shanghai Acrobats

Thursday, November 10, Shanghai

Morning Discussions in hotel with Shanghai education colleagues. Three groups met to discuss education administration in Shanghai, teacher training in Shanghai, and education in the United States.

Afternoon Visit to Chiaotung University

CHANG Shou, Vice Chancellor of the University
TSAO Ch'ung-hsieh, Dean of CU Faculty
CHIN Chueh, Professor, Shipbuilding Department
WANG Tuan-hsiang, Professor, Radio Transmitter Department
HSU Cheng-chih, Professor, Radio Transmitter Department
CH'EN Tsao-neng, Professor, Machinery Department
KAO Ming, Professor, Metallurgy Department
HSU Hai-kuo, Professor of Political Studies
HSIEH Shih-shun, Professor of Electrical Engineering
YU Chueh (f), Teacher of Electrical Engineering

Evening Banquet in honor of the delegation at the Shanghai Mansions, top floor. Madame LIU Fang, principal host.

LIU Fang (f), Chairman, Shanghai Education Bureau

Friday, November 11, Shanghai and Canton

Morning Visit to Huang-tu People's Commune (preschool factory)

YANG Hsia-yin (f), Revolutionary Committee Chairman
PAI Ming-an, Middle School Principal

Afternoon Walking, shopping, and sightseeing along the Shanghai Bund

Evening Flight to Canton

Arrival and Welcoming

CH'EN Ta-ching, Responsible Person, Canton Province Education Bureau Office
LIN Shou-chih, Canton Province Education Bureau Worker
CH'EN Chien-ya, Canton Province Education Bureau Worker
TENG Huai-ching, Canton City Education Bureau Worker
HUANG Cheng-yang, Canton City Education Bureau Worker
P'ANG Chung-hua, Interpreter, Canton Foreign Language Institute

Saturday, November 12, Canton

Morning Visit to Jan-he People's Commune and Ya-Hu Primary School

YEH Hao-shen, Commune Revolutionary Committee Chairman
NIU Hsiao-jung, Principal of Ya-hu School
LIEN Tsao-hung (f), Commune Office Director
WU Po-chou, Commune Office Worker
YANG Chien-p'ing, Vice Principal of the Ya-hu School

LI Hsi-hai (f), Vice Principal of the Ya-hu School

JUNG Ping-kuang, Canton Education Bureau Worker

WAI Huai-pan, Canton Education Bureau Worker

Afternoon   Visit to the Canton Trade Fair

Evening   Performance of minority nationalities folk dancing and singing

Sunday, November 13, Canton

Morning   Visit to Peasant Movement Institute

Afternoon   Discussions at Tung-fang Hotel with Canton education colleagues. Two seminars were held; one on education in the United States, a second on education in Canton.

Evening   Banquet at the Northern Gardens Restaurant in honor of the delegation; LIANG Ming-chung, principal host.

LIANG Ming-chung, Leading Member, Canton Province Education Bureau. Madame Chang Tsao-ch'ing of the Canton Municipal Education Bureau was also on hand to host.

Monday, November 14, Canton to Hong Kong

Morning   Train to Hong Kong Border

Members of the Delegation

Delegation Leader

    Dr. Ralph Tyler, Center for the Study of Democratic Institutions, Chicago, Illinois

Deputy Leader

    Mr. William A. Delano, Center for Global Perspectives, New York, New York

Delegation Members

    Dr. Gregory R. Anrig, Commissioner of Education, Department of Education, Boston, Massachusetts
    Dr. Adrienne Y. Bailey, Vice President, National Association of State Boards of Education, Chicago, Illinois
    Mrs. Grace C. Baisinger, President, National PTA, Washington, D.C.
    Dr. Mary Berry, Assistant Secretary for Education, Department of Health, Education and Welfare, Washington, D.C.
    Dr. Marlin L. Brockette, Commissioner of Education, Texas Education Agency, Austin, Texas
    Dr. Frank B. Brouillet, Superintendent of Public Instruction, Olympia, Washington

Dr. Calvin M. Frazier, Commissioner of Education, Denver, Colorado

Mrs. Richard D. Macy, President, California PTA, Los Angeles, California

Mr. Wilson Riles, Superintendent of Public Instruction and Director of Education, Sacramento, California

Dr. Thomas C. Schmidt, Commissioner of Education, State Department of Education, Providence, Rhode Island

Mr. Louis R. Smerling, President, National Association of State Boards of Education, Minneapolis, Minnesota

Mrs. Lillian Weber, Director, Workshop Center for Open Education, City College School of Education, New York, New York

Interpreter-Escort

Professor Ronald Montaperto, Department of Political Science, Indiana University, Bloomington, Indiana

Delegation Secretary

Jay Henderson, Program Associate, National Committee on U.S.-China Relations, New York, New York

State Department Escort

Donald Ferguson, Deputy Director, Office of East Asian and Pacific Programs, Bureau of Educational and Cultural Affairs, Department of State